38 at Estelle

Seeing the Unseen like Jesus

James Levi, Ph.D.

Cover design: Lifexcel Leadership Series Publication
Published by: Lifexcel Leadership Series Publication,
P.O Box 953 Huntsville, Texas 77342

For Worldwide Distribution, Printed in the U.S.A.
1 2 3 4 5 6 /18 17 16 15

For more information, please contact: Lifexcel Leadership Series Publishing at lifexcelleadership@gmail.com

ISBN: 978-1-7344551-3-7

DEDICATION

To *Saakshi,* our firstborn daughter, delight of our lives. Your passion, your insight, and your love make me attempt to follow your dance steps every day.

38 at Estelle

A very good work on the story of Bethesda by James Mathew. So many facets of the story that made me to examine it with a new set of eyes. It is well-written and organized as well as a challenging and an encouraging book.

Shawn Stutz
Author of *I Have Ears*

This is the best exposition of this passage I have ever read or heard! James Mathew is a great storyteller and his ease of language and imagination shines through.

Mathew P. John, Ph.D.
Founder, *Focus Infinity*

After reading this book, you will come away with many powerful lessons to apply to your own precious mortal life. This book has the power to set you free from whatever imprisons you — and once healed, to life afresh.

Ken Shelton
Author of *Leadership Excellence, In Search of Quality* and other titles.

This is a rich and powerful book! The Spirit of Jesus Christ shines brightly in this book and in you.

Helen Bass
Author of *Initial Reaction*

CONTENTS

PREFACE

Estelle, located in Huntsville, Texas, is one of the largest state prisons of the Texas Department of Criminal Justice (TDCJ). It is a complex prison unit comprised of over 3,000 offenders, and it also has a high security unit which houses some of the most violent male prisoners in the state.

This book highlights my personal experience of seeing the effects of human suffering, loss, and brokenness at one of the most suffering, lost and broken places: Estelle. Being a Christian minister for the last fifteen years has allowed me to witness the struggles of many hearts at various places and stages of life. Yet nothing had prepared me for the raw, intense and rough fight for the human soul inside the penitentiary and its ripple effects within the community. From these places of darkness emerge the stories of those who have been touched, healed and transformed because of an encounter with a certain rabbi and teacher. A teacher, who saw, learned, asked, and changed a life, touched a human, redeemed a community, and healed the world when he met the man who lay paralyzed for thirty-eight long years at the pool of Bethesda.

In this book, the narrative of the man from Bethesda is examined closely to understand the world in which he belonged to and the world in which he could not belong. This ancient scripture passage unfolds the fears, selfishness, and injustice that surround our lives within and without, and invites us to live like Jesus Christ, the Teacher.

ACKNOWLEDGMENTS

I want to express my thanks to all those who believed in me in making this project a reality and traveled with me on my spiritual journey. I am grateful for the excellent leadership that I was blessed with at Estelle, the Texas state prison. I want to thank the administration and the staff for their support and encouragement that helped me see the work of God in the midst of brokenness, violence and suffering. I have been greatly blessed by the life and stories of many of the inmates, who have helped me to see God in a very powerful and tangible way.

I want to thank the editors for making it easier for the readers to see the one who is at work in unexpected places. I also want to thank my parents (and my parents through marriage) who attracted me to follow Jesus Christ and to be a Christian minister by modeling lives of sacrifice and love for the people lying at the pool of Bethesda.

I am grateful for my wife Annie for her unconditional love and for her daily encouragement. Thank you.

The Feast of the Jews

After this there was a feast of the Jews, and Jesus went up to Jerusalem. Now there is in Jerusalem by the Sheep Gate a pool, which is called in Hebrew, Bethesda, having five porches [colonnades]. In these lay a great multitude of sick people, blind, lame, paralyzed, waiting for the moving of the water. For an angel went down at a certain time into the pool and stirred up the water; then whoever stepped in first, after the stirring of the water, was made well of whatever disease he had.

Now a certain man was there who had an infirmity thirty-eight years. When Jesus saw him lying there, and knew that he already had been in that condition a long time, He said to him, "Do you want to be made well?"

The sick man answered Him, "Sir, I have no man to put me into the pool when the water is stirred up; but while I am coming, another steps down before me."

Jesus said to him, "Rise, take up your bed and walk." And immediately the man was made well, took up his bed, and walked.

And that day was the Sabbath. The Jews therefore said to him who was cured, "It is the Sabbath; it is not lawful for you to carry your bed." He answered them, "He who made me well said to me, 'Take up your bed and walk.'"

Then they asked him, "Who is the Man who said to you, 'Take up your bed and walk'?" But the one who was healed did not know who it was, for Jesus had withdrawn, a multitude being in that place.

Afterward Jesus found him in the temple, and said to him, "See, you have been made well. Sin no more, lest a worse thing come upon you." The man departed and told the Jews that it was Jesus who had made him well.

For this reason the Jews persecuted Jesus, and sought to kill Him, because

1

He had done these things on the Sabbath. But Jesus answered them, "My Father has been working until now, and I have been working." Therefore the Jews sought all the more to kill Him, because He not only broke the Sabbath, but also said that God was His Father, making Himself equal with God (John 5:1-18 NKJV).

INTRODUCTION

The heavy metal gate behind me clanged shut. The sound grated on my ears and reverberated through the hallway. Standing in the abandoned parking lot, I once again looked behind me at the heavily guarded penitentiary that houses thousands of offenders. Each of them has a story, each of them had promise—but many seem empty and are living a life best described in prison slang as "maintaining"—or just trying to do the best under the given circumstances.

This night was unusual. It was not just the darkness outside or the surrounding silence that bothered me, but the slow yet clear words that were uttered from the quivering lips of a middle-aged, sharp looking man with carefully combed hair that seared my heart. He said, "Today is my mom's birthday and in my father's house there are many rooms and in the large dining room there is my chair, where I always used to sit when my family gathered to celebrate..." He paused for a moment, "But after so many years being away, the chair is *empty* as I have been missed, almost forgotten and carefully hidden from the rest of the family." Then he looked away and stared at the blank wall behind me.

As a pastor, I often sit with people who have gone through serious life challenges that sometimes make them feel both small and invisible. Still, this man didn't appear to be unseen. He had a good spirit, depth, and openness. As I sat and listened to him that evening, I heard for the first time what it takes to make a living human disappear. To snuff out a man of promise. For a celebration to be incomplete. For potential to be hidden—leaving an *empty chair* behind.

Here in the life of this man, we will see the story of a large, powerful system and community at play. In recognizing this fact, we are confronted with our own human fragility, our spiritual depravity, and our own pain. I discovered the striking parallel, the surprising similarity, and the strange connection of this man's life to a long-ago event that happened in a hidden community in the land of old Palestine, at a place called Bethesda. A place that was uncovered by a young rabbi who discovered there a man who was lost, forgotten, and hidden for thirty-eight long years—and who reached out and recovered humanity from its brokenness and endless suffering.

Now, please allow me to introduce you to Tim, the man who opened my eyes to see the empty chair.

The Life of Little Tim

Tim grew up in a home that demanded perfection and expected excellence in all things, especially in academics. His parents were well-known and reputable educators. They placed pressure on Tim and his younger sister, Chelsea, to perform at a level much higher than others. In his early academic years, Tim managed to do well because his hyperactivity was controlled by fear.

He had a slow growth spurt and so was nicknamed "Little Tim" by his teachers, but that changed in his late teenage years as he grew tall and lean. As years passed, he found it very hard to concentrate and be tied down to a specific task. His parents put money into various tests and costly treatments, but they did not help. To their embarrassment and heartache, he was often labeled "uncontrolled" and a "slow learner." He frequently got into trouble for breaking the rules at school and instigating fights with kids on the streets.

His sister, Chelsea, performed much better and was laser-focused in achieving everything her parents dreamed of for her. There was nothing stopping her. Chelsea was enrolled in different skill enhancement and language development programs that would give her that extra edge and ensure her acceptance by an elite college. She, as well as her parents, knew that her future was secure and bright as a morning star. But their daily concern and fear was for Tim and his constant battle with everything at school and life in general. There was nothing they could offer to help. He was hard-headed, unbridled, and insubordinate for most of his teenage life.

Though his parents were prominent and highly respected members of society, the issue with their son was a black mark that they failed to come to terms with. For Tim, life was quickly spinning out of control; he could not prolong his studies anymore and found refuge among those few friends who, like him, had nothing to look forward to in life. This bunch of teenagers regularly experimented with various illegal activities and did not feel a bit of guilt when it came to bending any rules. They were bonded rather loosely, yet were strong in their purpose. The way they found meaning in life was by forcefully trying to defeat the system they believed had made them outcasts. They were living life in the fast lane—each of them had a deep desire to a *live*—even if their lifestyle only made sense to them. It didn't matter anymore how their actions affected others.

Initially their unruly behavior started with petty offenses, but soon escalated to well-organized crimes. The puzzle for many remained—how could a young man growing up in a good, well-educated home find himself cruising through the night searching for innocent victims to steal from, kill and destroy? His parents weren't surprised when they found out that their only son was arrested for being part of a grave crime. Tim wouldn't be coming home for a long time.

Prison Life

Growing up was tough for Tim, but nothing could prepare him for the iron-barred cell he was about to enter. He was shipped to one of the worst prisons in the entire state, where life was reduced to survival of the fittest. He quickly found himself thrown like a lamb among wild beasts determined to devour him. Every minute was filled with fear until he decided to conquer the very thing that made him cower. He became aggressive, always on the offense, out-of-control and, angry. All his fears transmuted into anger, which was released when he picked fights with other inmates and hurt them, gaining him acceptance, respect, and much-preferred isolation. The other inmates eventually left him alone, and he wanted it that way.

A prison or penitentiary, of course, cordons off offenders from the general population, hiding them from the public's eyes and making a "normal" life impossible. At the same time, it is the place where all the once wanted, now despised ones gather, hoping to make sense out of their caged lives, brokenness and hopelessness. There is no smooth or straight road back to society. The common saying is, "Once a felon, always a felon." That's how many in society see them, brand them, deal with them, firmly believe and imagine them. There is no place for them "out there" or "in there"—only a miracle can set them free, and miracles in their minds are rare and reserved for the few that are favored.

Tim may have survived among the beasts of the prison system, but the darkness and craziness around him kept him from really living. He was certain he'd never find meaning in life again. In his fight for survival, he had created a whole new identity that made him more comfortable at the *poolside,* as we will see later in the story from Bethesda, the place where society's sick lived.

***

During this late-night meeting in the unit chaplain's office, listening to Tim's story, I realized that the description of this person and his past didn't match the present. In his deep voice he told me what kept him alive through the years was something beyond his strength or power. It was something beyond what a prison could ever offer. As I was listening, I could not bring myself to think that a life like his could ever make sense, especially when things around him were so dark and insane—and things within him seemed so hopeless. I will never forget what Tim said:

"It happened about seven years ago, I was thirty-eight years old then and had been locked for most of those years and thus I had given up on life. In my hopelessness, I met someone in my dark, lonely cell who made me walk…when I thought I had no strength or life left in me to take even one step forward."

Sitting there quietly and listening to those words, I knew I had to hear more.

A man being removed from everything he knew because he wasn't able to play by the rules, found himself in a place where the *invalids* of society are quarantined. There he found a survival method that is hard to endure unless you are one of the favored ones, the ones who have the connections to pull strings, those who are able to beat the system, or ones who are strong enough to overpower all.

His struggles brought him to a place where he gave up on life and just survived by breathing every day, staying under the radar and keeping his nose clean. His life would remain that way until his thirty-eighth year, after a strange encounter with someone indescribable, someone more than a man. The one who saw him, asked about him, healed him, and journeyed with him. Someone who was interested in getting to know him the way he was, talk to him and walk with him. one who would change everything for Tim and the world he now knew and lived in.

I didn't realize that this half hour would stretch for such a long time and unfold into an intimate and spiritual conversation. I don't know why, but I was sensing that the darkness of the night outside was shrinking back at the flickering light of his story. Right there I could clearly see in his story, what the man who once lay in a place called Bethesda some time ago had gone through (John 5:1-18).

Allow me to take you back in time but forward into understanding the human heart and the art of living…living according to the rabbi—the teacher—who saw, learned, asked, spoke, walked, and changed an individual, a community, and the world.

This book is more than just Tim's story—it is the story of many who find themselves to be "abnormal" and cannot fit within the demands of the community and/or fail to navigate within the guidelines that society enforces. This is about every tear that falls when trying to make sense of the brokenness within and without. Many are slowly cast away, forgotten, lost, and hidden. They are never heard again, their stories are forgotten, their chairs remain empty while the rest of us are there at the table enjoying the feast.

Introduction

Hidden underneath is a greater story of the one who is able to walk into every dark and seemingly hopeless place and search for those who are lost, forgotten, hidden, and hurting. This story takes a deeper look into the pain and suffering of those who are rejected, ignored, and neglected because they do not belong. It also reveals the dark truth of those who, with their powers and resources or connections, have kept the weak and poor pushed to the edge, marginalized and deprived of their rightful share.

This book uncovers the colonnades, or hidden porches, of the communal, religious, and political structures that keep the frail, unfortunate, and disabled sidelined. The truths in this book reveal how life can be restored and how every soul can find purpose and meaning that bring healing and lasting transformation within a community—within hearts and minds. I will share stories and seek answers. This book does not offer a historical or theological explanation. Instead we will look into an ancient story in the context of the reality of the world we live in.

I sincerely pray that you may be able to see in the following pages a reflection of your life, or maybe the lives of your loved ones, or your community. And my heartfelt desire is that you may have a personal, divine and unique encounter with Jesus Christ, the rabbi and the teacher,. May your eyes meet the compassionate eyes of the one who searches out every human heart and invites us to get to know him. He is the one who celebrates a rich feast, a feast that brings the community to its rightful place.

Thank you in advance for sojourning with me to the feast of Jesus, the one who truly fills the empty chair. Come with me as our present life joins with the ancient story from the sacred text. Let's unearth the beauty, meaning and life from under the covered porches of the dusty and dirty place called Bethesda.

CHAPTER ONE

FEAST AND THE FAITHFUL

If you don't know what you're living for, you haven't yet lived. –Rabbi Noah Weinberg

When I attended seminary in Pasadena, California, I often visited various places of worship. There in the foothills of the mountains is a beautiful Passionist retreat center with a charming chapel where faithful Catholics meet regularly on Tuesday mornings for mass. Sometimes I would go there and sit on the beautiful deck near the mountain overlooking the panoramic view of the City of Angels, and enjoy a few moments of serenity and solitude. I would experience peace that comes with being alone in nature and beholding God's amazing creation in silence.

Then I would emerge from the stillness. I frequently visited the Jewish synagogue where two weekly services were held: Friday evening Shabbat and the Saturday Sabbath service. I also enrolled in a Hebrew class held in the temple to learn from a scholar who had grown up in Israel.

But none of my visits to the synagogue compared to the time when we neared the grand feast of the Jews. Even as a Gentile who was not very familiar with their religious calendar, I could feel the excitement in the air as they approached their joyous festive season. I heard the children speak about the fun activities they would be involved in and eagerly await the sweets they would eat. There was grandeur and anticipation when elderly women talked about the delicious meals they were going to prepare for the community, and the young women talked about the fashionable clothing they were going to wear. It was a communal spirit, with participation and preparations among both young and old.

Although they are thousands of miles away from their promised land, these Jews still come together as a community and celebrate the feasts. The busyness and individualistic lifestyle of the Western world, which many of them have adopted as their second home, does not dampen or deter the spirit of the festivities.

This made me wonder...If these followers of the Law of Moses observe the feasts with such reverence and earnestness, even after many generations and much distance from their homeland, how much more festive the mood must have been in the old Palestinian streets when and where a young Jewish rabbi, the teacher named Jesus, walked and talked among them. The feasts had significant personal, spiritual and communal meaning.

Since the healing of the man at Bethesda, described in John 5:1-18 at the beginning of this book, revolves around the feast of the Jews in first-century Jerusalem, we need to understand the significance of the feast from their cultural perspective. What did the feast represent for an ordinary Jewish family living in Palestine at that time? It would definitely be much different from our modern way of celebrating holidays, which mostly consists of shopping, gift-giving, partying, and entertainment.

Descriptions in the ancient scripture give us a glimpse into the feasts of the Jews celebrated in old Jerusalem. The ancient Jewish feasts have relevance, significance and meaning, and speak fresh, powerful truths to us today. Their celebration highlights some unique cultural and traditional ways in which a community celebrates freedom, faith and family, faces failure and fear, and embraces their fight for life. In the following chapter we will take a closer look into how this ancient story of the Jewish feasts uncovers some hidden truths of our lives in this day and age.

Five Observations

The feast of the Jews has a distinct flavor and color that can be seen even in the dark night as any stranger in town walks through the brightly lit streets of old Jerusalem. It can be heard at a distance; the captivating folk music being played and the children dancing to its tune. And it can also be intensely felt in the small conversations of the villagers at every street corner as people sip their evening tea. It is a communal affair embedded in a deep traditional and religious history. These people, over many generations, have gone through various places and seasons; they lived as nomads and occupied the Promised Land, they ruled and they were exiled, they owned and then they lost everything, yet they maintained their individual identity, distinct culture and lifestyle, a united front and a unique way of celebrating the feast.

Here I highlight five distinct observations associated with the feast of the Jews: freedom, family, religion, business, and politics.

1. Freedom: The Jewish feast was an expression of freedom. Jews who lived in Jerusalem knew how to celebrate. Feast days had a very different feel and look from the ordinary days of the year. The whole *land* often appeared to be rejoicing along with the people who were celebrating. The celebration affected everyone—no one was exempt. The poor would save whatever they could to join with the larger community, while the rich would spend enough to stand out from the crowd. Kings invited officers to the feast and gave gifts to their guests.

One of the distinctive traditions practiced was that during this time a convict chosen by the crowd would be set free (see Matthew 27:15). Hence, it was a time when people could exercise their freedom as well as to bring freedom to others. Feasts even under oppression and colonization gave a taste of freedom. The feast symbolized freedom from bondage and imprisonment—a time that united people. No one would want to miss the feast, a fun-filled time of the year.

Many people looked forward to this time as it gave them meaning and purpose in life. For them, life was meant to be celebrated and enjoyed, and the feast fulfilled that desire. The feast of the Jews catered to every age group. It helped many of them forget the difficulties of life. Older folks didn't remember their days of war, women for a moment could enjoy freedom from societal pressures, and young ones could take off from their long days at temple schools as they all reveled in the celebratory mood. During the feast, all could ignore their worries, enjoy themselves, and experience a greater degree of freedom—the deep desire of every human heart and community.

Looking at the feast of the Jews from outside, it would be hard to tell if there was anything actually missing. But looking from inside, within each life, beneath all the glamour being played out at the feast, it would not be difficult to tell that true freedom was missing from some homes and some lives. Those who were experiencing the pain of missing their loved ones, especially during the feast, were constantly reminded by the empty chairs at the dinner table.

But if these suffering ones had the freedom or courage to voice their pain aloud or express their anger for the sake of those absent, would it truly be heard or would it fall on deaf ears? Or be drowned out by the other noises of the feast? Difficult questions often unasked by mainstream media or civic leaders in those days, as well as now, are: What price are people willing to pay for freedom? Or is freedom meant exclusively for a certain group? Are there some who are being held back from experiencing freedom and thus are missing from the feast? Where are they, if not in Jerusalem, during the feast of the Jews?

2. Family: *The Jewish feast was a time of family reunion.* It was always a family event. Families would eagerly look forward to this time of fellowship. Feast time was an excuse for extended families to come together to celebrate each other. Many who were away from their homes made travel arrangements ahead of time to be with their families during the feast. A feast without all the family present would be incomplete.

The gospels describe the time when Jesus was twelve years of age and his family traveled to Jerusalem to celebrate the feast along with the whole village. Often the feast brought the entire village together, highlighting the high priority Jews had for their own people and for uniting them. For some, the feast also created tension and difficulties that often come with family gatherings. Certainly reunions involve a lot of family talk, food, games, kids, and showing off new clothes and fashions. But there are also some intense yet brief discussions and a few stories that families carefully avoid because they are painful reminders of those whose chairs are empty.

But when those empty chairs were spoken of, many things were uncovered—and some at the feast were unprepared. Questions came to mind such as: Why were there some stories or some people missing from the large family dinner? Can family still remain a family when some of them are missing or a few are absent from their chairs for some time? Why is a family still able to carry on normally when there are those unaccounted for? Where are they, if they are not in Jerusalem during this feast of the Jews?

3. Religion: *The Jewish feast was a time of high religious activity.* Most religious Jews of that time would come to Jerusalem, since the city was the center of religious life for them. The feast of the Jews was a time of celebration and fellowship as well as fulfilling religious requirements mandated by the teachers who interpreted the law. Jerusalem had the temple, and people came from all over to worship God. For the Jewish people, the celebration of the feast was not just a custom—it was a command. Their scriptures required them to be in the temple, to be a part of the feast; to be absent meant disregarding their faith or rebelling against religious obligations. So people participated with much fervor, signaling their unique election as the chosen people. The book of Acts of the Apostles highlights the time during the feast of Pentecost, when Jerusalem was filled with visitors from around the world.

Faithful Jews traveled to Jerusalem to be with their people in their own land. To be considered pious or religious, a Jew had to make the trip to Jerusalem during the feast from wherever he or she was at the time. Presence at the feast also opened doors of acceptance among the faithful, enabling participants to carry out many things that nonreligious people could never accomplish outside the temple.

For visiting outsiders, the feast would look very attractive, it might give an impression of God-fearing, scripture-loving, law-abiding, holy people. It might even suggest that religion brings true blessings.

Upon a closer look, did it also in some way show the *pressure* of being a religious Jew in Jerusalem during the feast? Or did it favor only a certain type of religious people to be welcomed to the feast? Were there some from among the people who were missing these religious feasts because they weren't religious enough or didn't measure up to the standard set by the temple leaders? Or another good question to ask: Who even created such rules to shun people from being able to come together in the name of religion? Did the temple authorities became too powerful, marginalizing some as unreligious, or were there a few who acted wrongly in the name of God and the temple and took the authority on themselves? Why were some family members missing? Where were they, if not in Jerusalem during the feast of the Jews?

4. Business: *The Jewish feast was a time of business opportunity.* This event also created an economic boom as business people set up stores and small stalls for selling various wares to the public. The feast generated good profits, attracting large crowds. Jewish merchants knew how to exploit these opportunities, and they did not let profit slip away. The large crowds that came to the feast helped both the small and large businesses in the community. Some people sold pigeons to pious, religious folks; lambs and goats were up for sale, and others exchanged money for those who came from other lands. The feast of the Jews generated business opportunities, encouraged young entrepreneurship, and assured a financial boom. It was a progressive stimulus for a sluggish economy.

During the feast, every street was seemingly paved with gold, and every corner beckoned opportunity. Jewish religious leaders and shrewd businessmen also knew how to maximize their profits. Temple leaders had encouraged corrupt business practices as a way to profit themselves. The gospels give an account of this, when Jesus gets frustrated with those who were making the temple a place of business by harassing the poor. The feast of the Jews created opportunity for commerce and the economy to grow.

One question that was probably never asked by the temple authorities was: "Is it a fair trade?" Did the economy have the upper hand over the poor and deprived? Were the voices of the humble shut down by the powerhouses of the temple who got a cut of the profit? Was the profit shared by an elite few and the rest left to fend for themselves? Are these enterprises meant to make the wealthy wealthier and the poor poorer? Are there some who cannot make it to the feast because they cannot afford it? Where are they, if not in Jerusalem during the feast of the Jews?

5. Politics: *The Jewish feast was a national political stage.* Ambitious people prepared themselves for this event with great anticipation. They came together to meet with friends and relatives, for a time of camaraderie, and the festivity and activities gave an aura of excitement. In some way, it also satisfied the deep suppressed hunger of the oppressed Jewish tribes. These gatherings gave them an excuse to forget the realities of the oppression they were facing daily because of Roman tyranny. At the feast, they could freely express their voices in public and not be bothered by the authorities. The feast became an occasion that fulfilled the religious, social, political, business, and various other felt needs of the people. It was a place where Jewish people could share their communal pride and also protest against the injustice of the foreign government.

This was also a place for many to promote national ideas and engage in political debate and strengthen their religious power base. This gathering often served as a perfect platform for upcoming leaders to attract attention through their fiery freedom speeches delivered with messianic passion. For anyone with political aspirations or religious ambitions, it would be foolish to miss such an occasion. To be at the right place (with the right motive) at the right time (among the right crowd), meant to be at Jerusalem for this feast. For many Jews, the feast provided a step toward achieving their dreams, gaining power, and realizing their purpose.

Observing this aspect, an outsider might think this is the true meaning of the feast—but is there something meaningful missing? Was there true concern for every human? Or did this gathering serve only a few select groups who had their own personal or political agendas? Also, were there some whose concern was never mentioned, or were there more than a few who were forgotten by the leaders as well as by their own people? Where are those who are never mentioned by the politicians, if not in Jerusalem during the feast of the Jews?

***

From these observations of Jerusalem, the feast can look very attractive, exciting, and beautiful for the family, promising freedom to the nation, an exhibition of holiness to the faithful and religious, a passionate gathering of national leaders promoting a spirit of unity, free enterprise, business, and a promise of a better tomorrow. On the other hand, it also raises a very serious and curious question about the qualifications required to experience a good time during the feast. One wonders if some truths were being deliberately hidden from the public eye and pushed undercover.

Next we will follow the narrator of the gospel and his perspective from 2,000 years ago, as he moves us to the ancient streets and markets of Jerusalem and takes us into a very remote, untraveled, less-attractive location in the city, following the footsteps of a rabbi, the teacher. In the next chapter, we shall examine if all we see at the feast is all that there is to experience. Or is there more to the feast of Jews that can be uncovered?

CHAPTER TWO

HIDDEN UNDER THE COVER

What is true by firelight is not always true by daylight. –French
Proverb

Everything looked remarkably beautiful that evening at
the Harrington house. Guests were expected to arrive in one
hour, and Carter Harrington was on his way from his office in
his brand-new, shiny blue Cadillac. His wife, Jane, had come
home early to make sure everything was taken care of. The
maid went the extra mile to make sure that everything looked
and smelled perfect. The food was ordered from the best
caterers in town. Mrs. Harrington dressed her best that
evening. She picked up their two daughters a little early from

school on her way home. The candles were lit, the driveway was clear—everything looked inviting to all the special guests.

As a socialite couple, the Harringtons were well-known for their lavish parties, where they made sure that guests enjoyed themselves with the best food and drinks that Jane hand-picked from her favorite restaurant just down the street.

But this evening was extra special. The couple was celebrating their thirteenth wedding anniversary, and the invited guests were mostly immediate family and close friends, with one exception. Jane invited Michael Todd from the insurance firm where they both worked. Although Carter was not very keen on having him show up, he didn't make it an issue. But Mr. Todd stood out as an odd man among the company that evening.

Soon the house was filled with well-dressed, good-looking people, and the aroma of spicy appetizers was in the air. It was a great evening, except for the veiled tension between the celebrating couple. Was the celebration a cover-up to hide something? It was noticeable that there were fewer laughs from the hostess—one guest even made a remark about it—but that sentiment quickly faded as people enjoyed the new home and appreciated the fine interior decoration and exterior beauty.

As the guests slowly departed, they praised Jane for the great time. It was not until Carter put the two girls to bed and walked toward his bedroom that he noticed the manila envelope on top of his study table. Curious about the contents, he opened the envelope—only to get the shock of his life. His wife of thirteen years had just served him a separation notice. Was he caught off-guard, or did he just miss the signals? A month earlier when they were on a mini-vacation with the kids at the beach, Jane had mentioned that she didn't feel loved and wasn't sure that she loved Carter anymore. He wasn't sure where her comments were coming from, so he didn't take them seriously.

Tonight, the papers he was holding were real, and his mind was racing at a faster pace than he could even fathom at that moment. He couldn't believe his perfect life and his perfect family were going to collapse like a deck of cards right in front of his eyes. And the worst surprise of the night was the way Jane handed him the news. No explanation, just a ordinary-looking envelope strategically placed for him to find—alone. It was as if she had chosen to hurt him. Maybe she was battling some demon inside of herself and the only way she could get rid of it was to direct it at someone else— and she found him to be the person. She had planned the "surprise," and the timing couldn't have been more perfectly painful.

***

This story might seem like a script for a Hollywood movie if it had not happened to a good, God-fearing, church-going, "normal" family within the community. Passing by their home and peeking at the calm blue waters in the pool behind their white picket fence would never at any time have given any less than a favorable impression. How could everyone miss the obvious—are we all living two different lives?

This truth of missing the obvious is played out daily by people living in multimillion-dollar beach homes to those dwelling in a single-room basement. Lives appear one way from the outside, while harboring deep secrets and issues from an outsider. We are all skilled in advertising to the world and even to our near and dear ones that everything is just fine and as beautiful as the rising sun, even when we very well know that things are not as they appear.

The Harrington story is similar to the scene in the city of Jerusalem during the days of the feast. The city was decorated with every festive color, bright shining lights, the sound of bells ringing, accompanied by joyous music, topped with religious and traditional dancing. The celebrating crowd of both young and old overflowed and filled every busy market square. Yet, at the same time, the scripture focuses and forces our attention on a very different place within the city.

> *Now there is in Jerusalem by the Sheep Gate a pool, which is called in Hebrew,* **Bethesda,** *having five porches* (John 5:2).

The spotlight is now on that part of the city where no one wants to be—a place for the outcasts. The narrator turns our mind to Bethesda, which is surrounded by five covered porches, or colonnades. Were they purposefully covered? What happens if someone uncovers them? Is it allowed, or are there powers that will want to keep it hidden? Who is it that has the authority to uncover them?

Bethesda

Let us look closely into this place called Bethesda with the five covered porches.

1. House of Mercy: A gathering of the weak. Bethesda comes from a Hebrew word *khesed*, which means *mercy* or *loving-kindness*. Bethesda means a *house of mercy* or a *place of loving-kindness* where one finds mercy and hope. One would imagine this would be the sort of destination that is usually overbooked on most of the travel websites. This would be the place where people would prefer to go; but the truth we find as we uncover this *first porch* is that only the weak, homeless, diseased, and those forgotten from the feast are the ones found lying there, helpless, hopeless, and seeking mercy. The irony is that this painful fact is shielded from the eyes of the common feasting people of Jerusalem. Almost anyone would say there is always a need for God's mercy. Who wouldn't want more freedom in their lives? Who would say no to more mercy on any given day? Who wouldn't seek more faith? Are we isolating those who seek him and are left as unwanted? Are they seen as less fortunate and weak by the world and thus hidden or covered from the mainstream?

It appears that the people at the feast in Jerusalem required Bethesda to be covered, ignored, hidden, or kept from public view. Any visitor in Jerusalem at this time of the year would see all the colorful places and attend all the exciting events, buy lots of things, but would rarely ever go near Bethesda—the house of mercy. The town leaders also deliberately avoided this area during the festive season, since Bethesda had become a place of suffering and a pain-filled dwelling with disabled and sick people. Ironically, *mercy* was not much sought after in these dark corners of Jerusalem. It seems that either people did not need more mercy or they did not believe that mercy could be attained. They wanted to believe that everything was fine and that they could manage on their own. Was it their ego that kept them from admitting the need for someone bigger than themselves and their problems, or was it fear that kept them from being honest about their reality? A fear capable of pushing people to believe in self-sufficiency, when every morning the only thing they needed was new mercy in their life, family, and community.

When we fall into the trap of believing that mercy is optional or that it is meant only for those in desperate need, then we slowly and silently feel the pain of *mercy-starvation* or become *mercy-anemic*. This is mostly felt within our souls or inner world, since deep down we all appeal for mercy. Even though we might not admit it, we all have a profound need for mercy. Under the cover of darkness, many might take those slow small steps from the dark back alleys of Jerusalem to the lonely highway leading to the house of mercy, Bethesda. When our inner pain spills into the outer suffering and becomes too deep to be borne alone, a spark of inner strength ignites as the result of that small constant voice saying, "You need help...you need mercy, you don't truly have it all together, you don't have to hide it anymore, and you don't have to live like this."

Yes, initially a person moves along alone, but eventually others catch up. People find themselves in small groups, seeking out hurting companions and making their silent journey toward Bethesda. It is a place that is usually reserved exclusively for damaged or dysfunctional people. These outcasts are the only true family, and the only place where we sometimes find ourselves at home, where we can be true to ourselves.

When rest of the society is busy celebrating the feast and trying hard to put on a mask, decreeing to the outer world that "Everything is okay," while silencing the cry of the inner world that says, "Nothing is really working or okay." In the process, we get skilled in negating mercy, we try hard and soon grow clever. There is solace to be found in the house of mercy, for it offers genuine freedom to be ourselves, to take off the mask. It is a call to be who we are inside out, to be honest with ourselves and with others.

It's tough to face the fact that our lives won't always be easy, it is even harder to think that it is not going to turn out exactly the way we thought it might. This becomes a reality for many parents who have failed in raising their kids and for those kids who have turned out to be strangers in their own homes; for those whose jobs don't satisfy them anymore; and for those "friends" who don't want to move beyond connecting on Facebook or Twitter. It hurts to disguise ourselves or to pretend to be someone else.

After some time, we realize that we do not need to prolong the pretense, we do not have to live the lie that we are self-sufficient, maintain the facade of a perfect family, or try hard to look faithful and successful. For once, at the house of mercy, it is totally okay to be a failure, weak, and sick—now it is "normal" to be "not normal." How would you feel when you realize that no one is looking at you with those strange expressions anymore? No one expects you to be perfect at the place of loving-kindness.

Everyone is in some way, somewhere, and somehow broken, damaged, hurt, and in need of repair, in need of mercy. And there is a place where we can say it aloud without being shamed, without being judged and not even feeling guilty about it. We can be real with ourselves, real with others, and real with our pain. We can boldly look into the *dark night of our soul* and be still. We can lift up to the light our sins that have corrupted us and those around us. Apparently then that only happened in Bethesda…a place far from Jerusalem and hidden from those beautiful yet artificial lives; rich, powerful yet poor lives; strong, mighty yet weak lives—lives that perfected the art of masking.

It is a burden to live with deadness in us and not admit it; Bethesda offers a place to unburden ourselves of shame, guilt, and sin among those who are sick, disabled, and paralyzed— not just physically ill but perhaps emotionally, mentally, and spiritually impaired as well. Bethesda was then and is now a place for many where no sin is too big and no shame is too great. Bethesda is a community where we don't have to hide things to feel okay or normal.

How ironic it is that we often find refuge and acceptance among sinners rather than the righteous, and feel welcomed in the company of the broken. If this is true, and it is, then why do we put so much effort into acting as if we are perfect, and why do we strive so hard to be seen as better when all others need is a place of truth and honesty where they can bring their brokenness and pain? Why do we work so hard to shun those who are weak, when in their presence we find our own healing?

While during the feast Jerusalem appeared to be a place full of excitement, passion, and celebration, the weak, disabled, and sick were left out, confined to the company of losers at Bethesda, where misfits land and outcasts reside. For the celebrants, keeping company with those at Bethesda would dampen the spirit of feast. So reveling in the feast came with a price tag—the cost of living a false and fake life. Those few who had the courage to leave the feast and make their way to Bethesda were often shunned by the faithful. Their absence or empty chairs at the family dinner table would be ignored; and their stories would be omitted.

Scripture describes the people at Bethesda as "blind, lame, and paralyzed"—a place filled with pain and human suffering—and yet these people came with the hope of being healed and heard. They yearned to hear someone say they are not abnormal and it's okay to struggle with addiction, it is fine to be a chronic failure, their lives are not perfect, and even, perhaps, that it is normal to feel angry at God. They put away their reliance on self and stopped believing the lie that they could make it on their own—they came seeking the one who extends mercy to the weak and weary. In that process, they made the journey toward inner healing—a healing of the mind, body, spirit, and soul.

Scripture says that we should not hide our sins but accept and confess our iniquity before God and seek his mercy. One of the first kings of the united Israel made the mistake of hiding his shortcomings. Scripture says that King Saul did not humble himself; rather, he saw himself as strong, mighty, and unconquerable. The result was that his pride became the path toward his downfall.

David, on the other hand, was an ordinary shepherd boy who became king. King David admitted his crime of committing adultery and the cover-up murder of his own warrior. He knew he had sinned and acknowledged his faults and cried out to God for mercy. Later, although being a powerful king, he sought refuge among the weak, the failures, and the sinners of *Bethesda*. A place where there is hope for the lost, where the King of kings extends his hand of mercy and delivers all those who seek him and wait upon him.

We can do the same—we need to seek the one who is waiting for us to rely on him, trust him, and accept his mercy. We need to know that he came to heal the blind, lame, and paralyzed—in our minds, bodies, spirits, and souls.

The house of mercy provided them—and us—with a place where they could be who they were—broken and in need of healing. Bethesda often attracted courageous people who, because of their pain, could no longer subscribe to the fake lifestyle of society—they were forced to openly seek mercy. The irony is that society called them weak and sick, but the real weakness is when we hide pain. The true sickness of the soul is when we claim to be well enough to avoid being called a misfit or branded as a Bethesdaite or Bethesdian. Yes, the house of mercy was hidden from the lens of the feast, but it was very real to those in pain when the first porch is uncovered.

2. Sheep Gate: *Effects of a forgotten story.* A penitentiary is a daunting place where survival is not always assured. People often try to hide their weakness to appear strong until they face some real crisis and have to open up those deep, dark, hiding places.

As a pastor to prisoners, I have often sat with them in times of fear, sadness, and loss. I vividly remember when one young offender walked into my office, and I had to deliver the difficult news that his mother passed away. Some tough guys, even when they face such losses, remain calm, but this prisoner was different. He burst into tears as if a dam had broken from the pressure. I sat with him through that moment of pain and suffering; then to ease the tension, I asked if his mother had recently visited him in the prison.

He paused, wiped his tears away from his eyes, looked up, and said very softly, "Sir, I don't remember ever seeing her— she has been locked up in another prison since I was a baby." Just hearing those words made my heart skip a beat. I could identify with the hurt and pain of losing someone known, but how could I cry with someone who lost someone who was never there for him and whom he had never known. There was no mother in his life, but still he was mourning the pain of that loss.

Can we actually lose something that was already lost? Can we lose something we never had?

Between his sobs I could feel this loss was not of losing someone he didn't know—it was much deeper, it was about never having the opportunity of knowing someone who could have loved him and made his life a different story. The absence of a mother in his life created a hole, a vacuum in his life— there was no connection with the one who carried him in her womb, the memories of the one who gave him birth were missing. A mother who was there for a moment was gone, and now gone in a moment to become history. It was a story cut short. It felt as if his very belonging, his identity, his existence had been deprived from the very beginning because of the pain, anger, crime and punishment.

His tears were for the story of who he is and what he could be…the story of love, care, and nurture being snatched away in the initial years of his life by the cruel cycle of crime and addiction. Consequently, he lived the story he came to know on the violent streets that turned him into a career criminal. When he lost his own identity by growing up without a mom and dad, he picked up what was offered to him by his "homeboys."

> *Now there is in Jerusalem by the **Sheep Gate** a pool,*
> *which is called in Hebrew, Bethesda, having five porches*
> (John 5:2).

Does our society understand what it means when we forget the story of who we are and where we came from—and in that process do we lose ourselves and become somebody else? The story of Bethesda, as we uncover the *second covered* porch, addresses the story of a similar pain and suffering, hidden from or forgotten by the people in the feast.

Bethesda was near the *Sheep Gate,* a place through which animals passed into the city to be sacrificed at the temple. It was an unattractive place with the crazy noise of animals everywhere, a permanent whiff of dung in the air as well as dust that refused to settle. The livestock market just across the road was overflowing making it difficult for people to pass through it.

Travelers who were eager to make their presence visible among the feast-goers avoided this area. Clean and myrrh-scented tourists would only go to this place, full of the stink of animals, if they stumbled into it by accident or got lost. But to avoid this dirty side of the city also meant to ignore the truth or to purposely fail to understand the story that every sheep told as it was brought in to be slaughtered for the remission of sins of the people. In the better parts of the town of the feasting crowd, people would rarely have to live with the story of the lamb being taken through the gate or consider the price paid for every sin committed by individuals and the community, knowingly or unknowingly.

It was filthy in appearance, yet the sheep gate brought people closer to the truth of their own filth that was often unseen and undetected. These sheep entered the gate alive, but soon were laid dead upon altars for no crime of their own. They had to surrender their lives and be sacrificed for the sins of others. This bigger story was ignored and undermined by popular culture but witnessed daily by the weak, sick, and disabled population of Bethesda.

Was this story purposefully ignored, or did it become irrelevant to the celebrators of the feast? Was not the purpose of the feast connected with the deep truth of what was happening at Sheep Gate? Was not their identity as a nation connected to Abraham offering his only son Isaac as a sacrifice? Had they forgotten their usual rabbinic reading from the prophets, especially their prophet Isaiah who clearly detailed the events that were to occur concerning the Messiah who was going to be crushed for the sake of the people? And didn't the pioneers of the Old Testament faith practice the sacrificial atonement to be identified as a people and race chosen by the Almighty?

Now they cleverly avoided the dark but important aspect of the sacrifice in the name of freedom and progressive culture. Although hidden from the eyes of society, Bethesda still beckoned people to enter into the intimate story of their relationship with God. Though covered under the *second porch,* Bethesda still offered an opportunity to those sick and less-privileged to be drawn closer to their story. A story of God who from the beginning is seeking and searching for those who are lost as sheep gone astray.

3. *The Pool and the Angel:* *Living a life of expectancy and accepting the mystery.* Adjacent to the Sheep Gate was a pool of mystical power that attracted many people who were sick and disabled. Bethesda was known for its healing wonder, a place where disabled people waited for the moment when an angel moved or "stirred up the water." They waited for something to move in the water so that something could move inside them. Jerusalem, with all its colorful celebration and festivity, had removed people far away from the life of mystery, the unknown, and that which was beyond the natural. But at Bethesda, as we uncover the *third porch,* we find that it offers solace to weary hearts who know that life is more than a puzzle that can be solved by human inventions, ideas, or material comforts. Bethesda became a place too difficult to be comprehended or understood by the wise, healthy, and well-to-do citizens of Jerusalem. Rather, it proved therapeutic to those ordinary, weak, and lost ones who were able to accept the mysteries that life presents.

> *For **an angel** went down at a certain time into **the pool** and stirred up the water; then whoever stepped in first, after the stirring of the water, was made well...*
> (John 5:4).

When religion, business, and politics tried to come up with easy answers to life's tough questions, those at Bethesda were able to live with unanswered questions; they were okay living in that tension between what the natural and supernatural world offered. When science disqualifies the existence of the Supreme Being and young minds are trained to accept that which can only be proven and tested in laboratories, then we are cleverly distancing ourselves from a Bethesda experience of seeing the unseen, believing in the whole truth, and accepting our human fragility. Have we as a culture educated people to understand everything with only our minds? And when life doesn't make sense do we feel like failures, or are we bold enough to make space for people to accept mystery? Is there a place to recognize the sacred and to feel perfectly okay when found wanting and sit in that tension when there is no answer?

This irony of the feast of Jerusalem and the appearances of angels only at Bethesda suggests that we humans have limited control over the spiritual realm and its manifestations. We might create all the festivity in Jerusalem, yet we lack the supernatural power to produce an angelic stirring and healing. For that very purpose of experiencing the mystical, people had to move away from the feast and go to Bethesda—a sacrifice that only a few were willing to make. Whether the supernatural happens in ordinary places or ordinary people seek the supernatural, clearly the religious and celebrating crowd in Jerusalem was far from it. The more religious the people became, the more removed they were from the supernatural because that limited them to their natural senses.

The magical power of the pool of Bethesda also highlighted a truth that healing or angelic intervention was limited to a specific geographical location. The place and the time mattered. If you strayed away from Bethesda at the time of the angelic appearance, you missed the healing. You were qualified for the healing not because of the need, but by following the right protocol. The healing was attached to a place, and the place became famous for its healing. Why angels came to stir only the waters of the Bethesda pool is not explained in scripture, but it shows that they preferred that pool over others. Angelic visitations happened at an unannounced time, and so people waited and watched for the waters to be stirred for their healing. So it was not just the place but also the time that had become a significant element for the healing.

With all the supernatural events at Bethesda, there was something yet to be revealed or experienced that was beyond the time, space, favor, and even beyond anything that had ever taken place there. With everything that did happen in Bethesda and with everything that Jerusalem cared less about, there was still a deep yearning, a cry, and a waiting in every heart that desired something more, a larger truth—yet that cry seemed to go unnoticed and unfulfilled.

4. Competition: *A way of life.* I met Davis when he entered the regional medical facility of the prison where I worked as a chaplain. From the beginning I was impressed by his enthusiasm to be part of all the services and programs that took place in the chapel, especially because he was paralyzed from the waist down and had to be brought in a wheelchair. He was a friendly person and I was interested in hearing his story.

One day on my visit to the medical wing, I saw him sitting by his bed. He wasn't his usual self but still had the same friendly spirit. We began talking, and for the next twenty minutes, he described how he grew up selling drugs on the streets of a large U.S. city. He became successful, expanding his work as well as networking with various people in the city. He made a lot of money, married, and had three beautiful children. One night, according to him, he was at the wrong place at the wrong time and was the target of a drive-by shooting that left him paralyzed, though a few suspect the shooting was retaliation from the rival gang for cutting into their share. But he said that didn't stop him from selling drugs. His wheelchair become a cover and enabled him to carry on his business. But soon his act caught up with him, and he was locked up for a long time.

The day I met him, he was missing his three sons who were growing up without a father. He had been coming to the chapel and doing some serious soul-searching. That morning, with tears in his eyes, he said to me, "It's not worth it." All that he had done with his life, everything that he created, had brought him to a place where there was nothing left that he could call his own. He said that it was hard to live on the street, but even harder to live in this place.

"You need to have the right people at the right place and the right connections, and I now have none. Now all I have left is a past that hurts and a future that is dark. I'm looking forward to being there for my kids, but I don't think I can get out before they are grown up and gone," he said.

As I heard his story I felt that although Davis is off the streets and now wants to make his life better and is seriously considering changing his future, he feels there must be more than just a desire—he needs much more.

> *For an angel went down at a certain time into the pool and stirred up the water; then* **whoever stepped in first,** *after the stirring of the water, was made well...* (John 5:4).

At Bethesda, as we uncover the fourth covered porch, we find the sick, disabled, and blind people looked forward with anticipation and eagerness for healing and deliverance. Yet, there was a catch: not everyone received healing at the stirring of the water, only the person who jumped in first when the water was stirred. So, healing was dependent on speed. The healing favored the fast, the first, the resourced, and the *one who was at the right place at the right time.*

People missed out if they were late, slow, or had little support from others. It is ironic that these disabled people became entangled in the grip of fierce competition. They hoped that Bethesda would be a place where they could be accepted as they were. Instead, they were left out because they were too slow in stepping into the water. This affected their faith, hope, and future.

Was the spirit of Jerusalem slowly and cleverly invading and preying on the innocent and needy minds of Bethesda? Or are we all so selfish at our core as humans that after a while we just don't care about others—only ourselves? Would there ever be a resolution between those who make it and those who don't, and those who have it and those who don't, and the ones who are healed and those who are not healed? Did the healed always get appreciated, and were those who didn't get healed constantly rejected and left on their own to accept it as their fate? Or was Bethesda slowly accepting the culture of Jerusalem? Was there going to be a visitation of a different culture, something—or someone—greater than they had ever witnessed?

As we uncover this *fourth porch,* we find those who are trying hard to get their healing and find themselves again surrounded by the impossibilities of life.

5. Rejection: Living even when dreams are shattered. What happens when life constantly reminds you that you are not going to make it? How do you survive when failure and rejection are your daily meals? How do you tell others that one day your dreams are going to come to pass, when all you ever see are shattered dreams right in front of your eyes every time you make an effort? Can you convince others—or yourself—that next time it's going to be different? Is there an answer, or can you live without hope?

> *Now a certain man was there who had an infirmity thirty-eight years. When Jesus saw him lying there, and knew that* **he already had been in that condition a long time***...* (John 5:5-6).

Perhaps there are times when you think that this is your day, your time of healing. This time for sure you are awake, prepared, and you can even see the angel as it makes its approach; your eyes are fixed on its mighty white wings flapping and generating much wind and noise. It's a stunning scene to watch as it makes its smooth landing with a clear touchdown on the waters and slowly comes to a final stop with the simultaneous splash of your dive into the pool. You know for sure you are the first one...only to realize that you were a split second behind another one seeking healing. Your joy turns into mourning as you see a crowd ahead of you shouting victory for their loved one's healing. Who do you blame it on? Where do you hide your shame and anger? Is it possible to just bury it under the water? How many more rejections can you really handle?

Roberto's Prison Life: Roberto was not new to the prison system. Most of his life he had lived within the brick walls and behind the iron bars, handcuffed. In the past fifteen years of his life, he had been out in the free world for less than three months, the rest of it he has spent as an offender. He had gotten used to the prison environment, and now this was the only place he called home. Most inmates show excitement at the prospect of getting released and living a life of freedom, but for Roberto, being free was nerve-wracking and brought all kinds of fear and anxiety.

Roberto didn't know how to go out and create a new life. His greatest fear was that he would go back to the same lifestyle that brought him into prison in the first place. So he asked me, "Then why should I leave here, when I know I'm going to be back here anyways?" He is not wrong. For many offenders, prison is like a revolving door; they get out, and when they find that they cannot make it or adapt to the free world anymore, they commit crime just to be put back into the system again.

Most prison systems struggle with recidivism. It is hard for people who have experienced failure for so long to see that life can be better, that there is hope, and there can be a better future for them. Their minds cannot fathom those facts—for them life has been constant failure and rejection, so going out and trying to live life outside prison can be a daunting task. So many like Roberto, who have not known anything other than being prisoners almost their whole lives, come to accept life as it is and try to make meaning of it within their prison cells.

Similarly, fear of constant rejection paralyzes many lives in Bethesda. Life in Bethesda is for those who can move past their shattered dreams and can hold those pieces together and still remain calm. Right in the middle of the celebrations in Jerusalem, a shout from the rooftop announces to the whole world that they can live their dream lives, they can make it happen, if only they take the right steps. But as we uncover the last and the *fifth porch,* we hear a distant and different voice, the silent cries of those who still haven't made it, the hot tears of those who are still waiting for their breakthrough, the angry words uttered from the lips of those who have prayed for the healing of their young child for years and are still waiting. Those little weary bodies that have often gone hungry for days, hoping for food to calm their bellies on the streets of developing countries. As well as for those who have been locked up for years and desperately want to get out but know that's never going to happen. They still move on.

While Jerusalem hides the pain of those hurting and suffering from among their midst, under the fifth covering of the porch at Bethesda we find those who are still holding on, refusing to give up in the midst of suffering, pain, and shame.

Or maybe they have accepted this as their new lifestyle or a condition over which they have no power.

Although Bethesda is a place for the disabled, weak, and sick, the healing or deliverance comes for those who are able to get some help and find themselves prepared. Those who were not resourceful enough to arrive at the water first, ended up being depressed and hopeless in Bethesda, which was already reeking with anguish and suffering. These people have not only experienced the pain of their sickness, but also the pain of rejection. While the fastest or first one to dip into the water after the stirring is cured of her or his sickness, many others are left behind to pick up their own affliction once more and face new rejections.

For many, Bethesda, once seen as a place of deliverance, slowly became a place of rejection, pain, and failure, a place that pushes them to the brink of hopelessness. Their joy when they initially arrived has collapsed under the weight of repeated disappointment. When such rejection is experienced by many people at the same time, its magnitude increases, creating an environment of intense hopelessness and pessimism. For some, instead of bringing healing, the stirring of the water itself became a moment of fear and anxiety, triggering traumatic memories.

Where do you go from here, what do you do with such intense emotion experienced communally as well as individually? How do all these rejections affect the lives of those who have made Bethesda their residence—with no other choice?

Here we see two distinct sides and shades of Jerusalem and Bethesda, as two totally different places. One place is the site of the feast and people look healthy, are wealthy and enjoy family, freedom, and faith. They dream of a better future, yet are left with some unanswered questions. Deep down everything does not appear as pleasant as it looks on the surface. As the light fades from the street, the market square empties, and people gather back into the homes, while the dishes are being washed…thoughts of fear give way to panic; tears still fall, failures still haunt, and loneliness returns. Everyone may say that it is not legitimate or right to have these thoughts in Jerusalem, so they convince themselves these feelings are meant only for those in Bethesda. Those who are sick, disabled, and diseased are the ones who should be feeling afraid, lonely, and as if they are failures.

Second, there is Bethesda, a place where sick, paralyzed, and disabled people are lying in wait and in hope. Many cannot even pick themselves up and lack the basic freedom others enjoy. Few are visited by family. Some try to make the best of their situation and wait patiently, and yet they cannot help but end up discouraged. The only exceptions are those newcomers who move from Jerusalem to Bethesda when they are in pain and weak and those who walk away healed from Bethesda to Jerusalem after receiving their miracle.

So the traffic flows in a well-organized fashion, those who are sick go towards Bethesda and those who are healed go back to Jerusalem. Rarely did anyone who was healthy visit Bethesda from Jerusalem—until one man, a rabbi, the teacher named Jesus, made that extraordinary journey. He took the less-traveled path, walked against the current, took a countercultural step.

In the next chapter, we will explore why the rabbi, the Christ, traveled from Jerusalem during the feast of the Jews to Bethesda, a place of pain and suffering. What did he see that was unseen by many and how does that connect to a deeper meaning in the big story of life?

CHAPTER THREE

SEEING THE UNSEEN

We might be wise to follow the insight of the entrapped heart rather than the more cautious reasoning of the theological mind. —A. W. Tozer

As an aspiring medical doctor, Dr. Young Hu moved from Korea to the United States not looking for wealth and fame but wanting to make full use of his profession. He found a good opportunity in New York working as an assistant to an accomplished physician. He worked hard, made it through some tough challenges, and completed his residency at a prestigious medical school. Over the next twenty-five years,

Dr. Young Hu built his professional career and the kind of comfortable lifestyle that a good income could afford. As he approached retirement, he felt a deep desire to give back what he had received in his life. He looked for ways to serve people. Many of his friends were moving overseas to work with missions and nonprofit organizations. Some groups offered monetary benefits and adventure. He took some time off to seek God in prayer for the next course of his life.

He learned that near his home were many state penitentiaries and few doctors wanted to risk their lives to help inmates. These were places where hard-core criminals resided, and many people thought they were not worthy of living or receiving good medical care because they were dangerous. Doctors who took such jobs were at risk of being attacked and hurt, and were paid much less than their skills demanded. Even so, Dr. Young Hu felt that God was leading him to serve the people no one cared about.

One morning when I walked through his ordinary emergency room, an unruly inmate was being held down on the bed by four security officers. Behind all the chaos and commotion, I could see the compassionate eyes of Dr. Young Hu looking at this offender with a desire to heal and restore him.

***

I believe the strangest part of the Bethesda story is when we find Jesus near the pool. At this time in his public ministry, Jesus was growing in reputation and popularity. He attracted large crowds because his ministry was meeting the felt needs of the poor and needy all around Judean neighborhoods. Even without publicity, people were crowding his meetings. It was almost to the point that he had to hide in order to rest or have quiet time. There were many who came to him to be healed of blindness, lameness, and paralysis. All were coming to him; he didn't have to seek those who needed healing (see Matthew 12:15; 14:14). But we see him journeying away from Jerusalem to the highway leading to Bethesda.

He was not sick, and nothing indicates that he had friends or family in Bethesda who were sick. In fact, it was inappropriate for him as a rabbi to visit a place of disease, especially during a religious feast or ceremonies that would make him unclean for the occasion. Why did he follow a different agenda? What enticed him to leave the feast and mingle among the oppressed and neglected? This story speaks of the counterintuitive personality and the mission-infused life of Jesus. His servant leadership, his genuine spirituality, and his uncompromising lifestyle surprised many people of his time, as well as challenged the political, business, religious, and spiritual leaders. His life still continues to surprise and challenge us today.

*When Jesus **saw** him lying there and **learned** that he had been in this condition for a long time, he **asked** him, "Do you want to get well?"* (John 5:6 NIV).

There are five important and surprising observations of Jesus at Bethesda that model radical, simple, yet powerful principles for any spiritual leader or believer today to bring lasting transformation to his or her community, business, or family. The first three are mentioned in John 5:6 (NIV): *"When Jesus **saw** him lying there and **learned** that he had been in this condition for a long time, he **asked** him, 'Do you want to get well?'"* The last two observations are about Jesus who *healed* and Jesus who *walked* with the man again in the temple.

The spiritual leadership of Christ is characterized in these five words: *seeing, learning, asking, healing,* and *journeying.* These aspects shed light on how Jesus practiced his ministry and also invite us to see, hear, and ask for the stories of those whose empty chairs are found among our gatherings. We can fill those empty chairs through the ministry of compassion and courage.

Yes, Jesus goes to the feast, but then moves beyond the festivities in Jerusalem and takes that dusty, deserted road leading to Bethesda, on the outskirts of the city, where he saw, learned, and asked.

Jesus Saw

Jesus saw a paralyzed man at the pool—he saw what others missed, ignored, or didn't want to see. A good spiritual leader has good vision. Seeing is more than looking. Second Corinthians 5:7 in the King James Version says, *"We walk by faith, not by sight."* Vision, or what a spiritual leader sees, depends on the faith of the leader. Jesus walked by faith to the pool to a man who was paralyzed for thirty-eight years, rather than walking and taking in the sights and smells of the feast. His walk involved more than his personal aspirations or participating in the celebration; it involved being present to a man, being in the presence of a disabled, marginalized, and forgotten one—one who was purposefully ignored by the majority.

A different way of *seeing* or envisioning can bring about a big difference in a community as well as into our world, as evidenced when Jesus heals the paralyzed man at the pool of Bethesda, thus revealing the blindness of the larger community. After experiencing such a *seeing* among the disabled community, Henri Nouwen, one of the preeminent spiritual writers of his generation, writes in his book *In the Name of Jesus:*

> These broken, wounded, and unpretentious people forced me to let go of my *relevant self—*

the self that can do things, show things, prove things, build things—and forced me to reclaim that *unadorned self* in which I am completely vulnerable, open to receive and give love regardless of accomplishments.

Yes, seeing things differently is not easy, it requires more than our set of natural eyes, it necessitates a very different focus and faith.

Jesus exemplifies a missional lifestyle of being present in the moment, being led by the Spirit rather than the flesh, and walking by faith and not by sight. He is a spiritual leader who willingly submitted to compassion rather than self-aspiration or the pleasures of this world. What beckoned him from outside couldn't compete with what guided his vision from within. Jesus valued the purposes of God more than the praises of people. This story portrays a leader who stays true to his destiny rather than diluting his vision or getting distracted from his purpose.

Being at the pool of Bethesda was not the standard protocol or practice of a rabbi during the feast; but for Jesus, it was part of his purpose and his obedience to the will of his Father. He identified with his *purpose* rather than his *position*, which led him to see the reality of what was happening at the pool. Knowing one's purpose directs leaders to the right path or road that reveals what they need to see, which connects them to their destiny. Being true to ourselves—understanding our true self—leads to a place that demands our gifts be employed to fulfill our calling. If we are at the wrong place, we will not see what we need to see, we'll get distracted from our purpose and we will waste our gifts. Knowing who we are and what we are called to do will take us to the right place.

1. Jesus saw beyond the time. Jesus saw a paralyzed man lying near the pool waiting for healing for the past thirty-eight years, a sight which most of the religious, business, and political leaders, as well as the ordinary folks of his time, did not wish to see. For those leaders, *time dictated their sight,* and at that time it was natural for all to set their eyes and hearts toward the things that the feast had to offer.

The present culture appeals to the younger generation in a similar way. Many young minds are often attracted to things that are fun, famous and fast rather than being drawn to hard work, honesty and hospitality. There was so much to do during the feast and these things can require a lot of attention. For many, it was not the time to see sick people lying and waiting for their healing near a stinky pool. For them, this was the time when all the good things happened far away from Bethesda. But Jesus *saw* this man in spite of all the forces telling him to look the other way and focus on the things the feast could offer.

In her book *Strengthening the Soul of Your Leadership,* Ruth Haley Barton writes, "Spiritual leadership is the capacity to see the bush burning in the middle of our own life and having enough sense to turn aside, take off our shoes and pay attention!" She describes how Moses turned aside and saw something that ignited his life as the leader who brought deliverance to his oppressed people in Egypt—just as Jesus brought healing to the paralyzed man and deliverance for all of humanity. The burning bush can become a distraction if we are not sensitive to what the Spirit is doing and where the Spirit is leading us.

Similarly, for many who were in Jerusalem during the time of the festival, the sight of Bethesda was a distraction and troublesome place. It caused unnecessary deviation from the routine. But for Jesus, this was not an interruption but a necessity, a place that could not be ignored because it attached value to the human dignity of a man who had been waiting for healing for a long time. Bethesda was a place that for many was an unthinkable destination, but for a spiritual leader it was the birthplace for new and beautiful things.

Culture dictated that Jesus should enjoy the festive side of life, participate in the feast, and temporarily ignore any suffering. Yet, Jesus willfully committed himself to walking in the opposite direction. Being aware of worldly temptation, Jesus in the latter part of his ministry, when urged to bypass the cross by one of his close disciples, refused to do so. He was firm and focused and passionately moved toward his suffering to fulfill his purpose of dying for humanity.

The paralytic man who had been waiting for his healing for thirty-eight long years, along with his disabled community, were not only failing to attract any attention or interest from the celebrants of Jerusalem, but were deliberately blinded from their sight because it was not the right time. The feast had made the community very myopic and short-sighted; they could not accommodate the pitiable sight of pain and suffering with their celebratory mood, and so the best remedy was to remove themselves as far as possible from Bethesda.

During this time of feasting, the community's focus became negative toward anything other than joyous celebrating. This communal narrowing of vision can slowly remove hearts of flesh and replace them with hearts of stone. The heart that hardens narrows the vision of a community from being compassionate. That was what Jesus was pointing his finger at by leaving his footprints near the Bethesda pool during the feast of the Jews. He was knocking at the hardened hearts of the self-centered, pleasure-focused community of Jerusalem to open their eyes to those long-suffering.

There is nothing wrong with feasting in itself. In fact, it was a religious affair. Jesus himself went to the feast on many occasions (and was even accused of being a glutton; see Luke 7:34), but here he was able to highlight the dark side of the feast when people got caught up with life and failed to look and see beyond the festivities to those who were hurting, dying, and in misery. The life that ignores those who are suffering, those unaccounted innocent ones, and a culture that promotes only pleasure can easily miss the mark that God has for us.

Spiritual leaders need to see beyond what people want to show them and beyond what they are expected to see. The scene at this time of the year meant everyone should look at the festive side of life. Here celebration hijacked human compassion. People were giving into sensual desires, partying, enjoying food, music and fun. Jesus saw what most people did not want him to see. He was able to see the unseen and ignore the obvious. People can demand their leaders see many things that can distract them from their purpose. Leaders must realize this and never sacrifice purpose for position, compassion for popularity, and grace for authority. The example of Jesus teaches leaders to see beyond what is presented by the culture and those in authority. Leaders need to remember their ultimate purpose is to see what is hidden or unseen from view and un-see what often is attractively visible or seen by many.

Nancy & Her Patient

One late morning I was making my usual pastoral rounds at the hospital ward. As I was speaking with a patient, I heard a commotion in the adjacent room. I leaned my head out to see what was going on and that's when I saw Nancy running toward that room. Nancy was the main nurse on that floor, and I knew her very well. She had been busy taking care of many others, but she spotted this patient from afar who was showing some serious symptoms. While others were helpless at the sight of the patient's deteriorating condition, Nancy was focused on saving the man.

She ran to get the lifesaving emergency treatment to him as quickly as possible. She did not waste a minute, nor did she slow down. More importantly, even though she was busy with other things, she stayed focused on what others didn't notice. When things settled down, I met with Nancy and asked her how she saw what others had failed to see in the patient. She told me that she knew his medical condition as well as was aware of his family situation and some recent personal challenges he was facing, that had made her extra careful to watch him. A single moment of missed judgment from her could have left him in an unrecoverable position. Her willingness to *see,* even when things around her were demanding, hectic, and clamoring for her attention, saved a life that morning.

While walking back to my office, I was reminded of what could have happened if Jesus had ignored the sight of the man at the Bethesda pool or waited one more year or maybe even a few more days to go to him. Would the man still have lived or waited for his healing, or would he have missed it? Instead of making haste during the feast to see one man at Bethesda, if Jesus had just enjoyed the feast like the rest of the crowd, would the man still have been healed and returned to the temple, normal again? We do not have all those answers but one thing is clear, when Jesus saw the man who was not seen by the rest of the community for thirty-eight long years, his life was never the same again.

The rabbinic calendar required religious leaders to focus on the feast, but Jesus saw the man, in spite of tradition. He wasn't blinded by culture, religion, or any outside force. Jesus was moved with compassion, which gave him the sight to see what others failed to see.

2. Jesus saw beyond himself. During festive times, Jews tended to focus on what they would receive. For those seeking freedom, they experienced freedom during the time of the feast; those who were religious were involved in a lot of temple activities; those seeking family time enjoyed that; those looking to make some money by using the feast as a business opportunity did well; and even the politicians and aspiring leaders enjoyed success because of the receptive crowds during the feast. So, for everyone who came with their desires, the feast gave them an opportunity to fulfill them. They all looked forward to a great time of rejoicing, celebrating, worshiping, and enjoying the presence of God as well as time with each other.

It was not easy for Jesus, being a Jew, being part of a family, not to see what he had waited to see for a long time. It took great discipline for him to move beyond his own will and see for the sake of others. There were people waiting for him at the feast to promote his popularity and to promote the ministry—but he went beyond himself to see things that were not popular, yet were close to his heart. It moved him to see the needs and desires of a sick man at the pool. He put others' needs before his to see and feel what others felt. He understood those who were suffering and waiting for so long and entered into their experience.

In his book *The 21 Most Powerful Minutes in a Leader's Day,* John Maxwell says, "Leadership always has a cost. To be a leader, you may not be asked to leave your country and give up all your possessions, as Moses was. But leading others will have a price. Nothing is sacrificial unless it actually costs you something." On this occasion, for Jesus, *leadership* meant sacrificing his own fame and recognition to be present with a sick man.

To be led by the Spirit, every leader and every follower of Jesus should ask, "What is the sight waiting for me today, and what does it require me to sacrifice? What are people showing me this day, and if I focus on that, what am I not seeing?" Often, we only want to see and focus on our own needs, ambition, and desires; but in this self-centered process, we miss what God desires us to see—others' needs, desires, and dreams. This requires moving beyond ourselves. As a spiritual leader, Jesus demonstrated this great lesson of moving beyond himself.

Seeing the world from others' eyes can change our perspective. For those who were enjoying the feast, seeing the world through others' eyes would have disturbed their self-centered world. What if the businessperson on the streets of Jerusalem started marking down the product prices and gave up on making a high profit because he was seeing business from the eyes of the poor and needy who were not able to even afford the yearly sacrifices? What would have happened if the religious leaders of Jerusalem had seen the world from the eyes of the man at the Bethesda pool who was longing to be healed for the past thirty-eight years? Would they have waited long enough to postpone their visit to meet him?

Jesus inspired people to borrow a different set of eyes for the sake of a hurting world. He moved them to see the poor, lost, and needy with heavenly eyes in order to bring healing. It is significant that before the hand can heal, the eye must see. His act of healing the man at the pool opened the eyes of many, as well as touched the hurting world with the compassionate hands of God.

3. Jesus saw without fear. Many things are not easy to look at, and therefore, many people are afraid to look. Compassion demands commitment. Only a few people were willing to make that commitment to *see* what was happening at the pool of Bethesda. *Seeing* requires giving away what you want and taking on the burdens of others. Jesus, the spiritual leader was unafraid. He was willing to make that commitment and to face fear. He was willing to be disturbed by what he saw and also was willing to do something about what he saw. He was not afraid to see unpleasant things even when it demanded his very life at the end. The cross did not deter him from loving humankind. The crown of thorns did not prevent him from offering his precious life for the sake of saving this sinful world.

In her book *The Soul of a Leader,* Margaret Benefiel says, "Daring to dream is a part of choosing the path of a soul-based-leadership. Daring to dream involves stress and strain as well as joys and triumphs." Many people like to see the festive side of life because it does not require a commitment. They prefer the pleasure and joy. But choosing to see the difficult things, the way Jesus saw at the pool of Bethesda, requires losing oneself and doing something outside of one's comfort zone. Leaders are always committed to a cause that is greater than themselves and are willing to risk the sight that many purposefully ignore. Our master teacher, the rabbi, teaches us that a leader is someone who is unafraid to see because he or she is willing to give up their life for the sake of others.

Rabbi Jesus inspired a new generation of spiritual leaders to be a fearless people of commitment. The system and culture bought about by weak leadership focused on self-centered lifestyles. But Jesus dared the religious leaders to be unafraid of the sight of Bethesda. The people of Bethesda, for the first time, were able to look into eyes that were not frightened by the sight of sickness and paralysis but had the courage to believe in what God could do. Those burning eyes of a compassionate leader brought light where people's eyes had gone dim and warmth where their spirits had grown cold. God's representative appeared and his eyes sought out the world's weak.

Bill the Evangelist: Bill is a man who is passionate in sharing God's love with inmates in the administrative-segregation area, where they are separated for safety or as punishment. Often when I visit that part of prison, I see Bill standing outside a cell door praying for an inmate. I always melt at the sight of the heart of God beating fearlessly within this volunteer.

In the narrative shared in John 5:1-18, we can see Jesus' spirituality and leadership have a clear vision that define a destiny that fulfills God's mandated purpose. This passage also addresses the potential temptation that leaders often face, separating them from the purpose and destiny God has for them.

Questions to Ponder

*When Jesus **saw** him lying there and **learned** that he had been in this condition for a long time, he **asked** him, "Do you want to get well?"* (John 5:6 NIV).

1. Jesus saw beyond <u>time/religion</u>.

   What are the things that keep us from seeing what God wants us to see?

2. Jesus saw beyond <u>himself.</u>

   Are there any personal agendas that take us away from what God wants us to see?

3. Jesus saw beyond <u>fears</u>.

   What are some fears that keep us from seeing the way Jesus saw?

4. Jesus saw beyond <u>the crowd</u>.

   What does it take to see beyond the crowd and numbers and focus on one individual soul?

CHAPTER FOUR

THE VOICE

One of the greatest diseases is to be nobody to anybody.—Mother
Teresa

Growing up in a missionary home, Aasha Thomas knew
from an early age that her life was meant for something
significant. All the faith-filled messages and inspiring stories
she heard about early missionaries encouraged her to apply to
become a medical doctor. She didn't know that God was
preparing her for a different kind of service to meet a different
set of needs.

73

When Aasha was in the midst of her undergraduate studies, she felt the need to become a mental health professional and to serve her own people of India, who were often marginalized and neglected due to psychological disorders. A shame-based society often sees mental disease as a curse from the gods. Aasha could identify with these people who were suffering and being marginalized. She felt their pain and understood that she needed to learn more about the sicknesses and their conditions. It was a mammoth task since there were few resources and little research available in India where she grew up. To further her studies, she had to travel to the United States, which seemed an impossibility for her family because no one had ever gone abroad to study and for an average Indian it is very difficult to afford a Western education. She also knew that it would require many years of education to develop her skills as a clinician in order to be able to provide the best treatment plans to heal those who were suffering from psychological disorders.

It was a hard and long journey of faith and uncertainty, but she graduated and became a well-reviewed psychologist. She wanted to practice what she had learned and heal those who were hurting, but she felt that she needed supervision, which meant more time for what she was being prepared to do. She understood that healing comes when learning becomes part of the process. Faith requires one to involve in learning and walking that extra mile of God's preparation.

Dr. Aasha Thomas found herself now serving this community in a very different but powerful way. She never could have understood that her years of preparation and the experience of being uprooted from her own people would bring her to a place where God would use her to be part of the healing process of a community. A community where many of the students often experience the effects of prison life due to a family member or friend being incarcerated or maybe working for the prison system. Looking back, her heart is filled with gratitude for the opportunity of making a difference in young lives by extending the grace that she had experienced in her life. Her favorite story from the Bible that she often quotes is when Jesus meets a woman caught in adultery and extends grace when the whole society wanted to stone her. She says that "Only truth with amazing grace can do such an amazing thing within our community."

Moses and Paul are classic examples of two leaders who spent many years in preparation before their actual ministry began.

Jesus elevates the concept of *learning* to a higher level in this story of healing and justice. The healing of a disabled man was needed to bring justice to a society that was far removed from those marginalized and suffering people. Such understanding could come only by learning about the man who was removed from the community and also by looking at the society that exercised such power to keep him away. Jesus' presence at Bethesda marked a new chapter where he introduced a new concept of learning for the sake of healing, justice, and wholeness—the absence of which had made the feast empty, corrupt, and inaccessible for the underprivileged and unhealthy.

People often ignore the reality of suffering or mask its presence in society by being actively involved in learning that promotes the things they value—such as religion, family, business, politics, and the feast. Which in and of itself is noble, but becomes dangerous if pursued as an end instead of the means for a greater cause of serving God and his people. Jesus introduced a revolutionary and radical way of seeing the forgotten, the lost, and the victims of society and thus presented learning in a very different light. He intentionally used the time of the Jewish feast for his teaching moment to make a powerful point to impart a valuable lesson. He first involved himself in learning about an outcast, a disabled person living in a remote part of the city during the Jewish festival. His priority fueled the learning within the larger community and created an opportunity for that community to recognize victims of social injustice, corruption, and those affected by weak spiritual leadership, sin and darkness.

Jesus accomplished his purpose in three ways: 1) He learned by going to where the disabled man was and entering his world; 2) He learned why the disabled man was kept from the feast, then chose to heal the man and his society; and 3) He introduced learning to the feast to bring justice and wholeness to the community.

1. Jesus learned by going to *where the disabled man was, by entering his world.* Scripture says that Jesus *"learned that he* [the disabled man] *had been in this condition for a long time."* Jesus was willing to learn about the man, his condition, and about the duration of his suffering—learning with empathy, learning to understand others first, learning to understand the situation, and the extent of the suffering. Jesus shows the best way to learn is to be present with those who are suffering, engaging in their world of pain or failure, allowing the presence of defeated, disturbed, divorced, and suffering people to teach him what the temple and the community's festive spirit failed to teach. Jesus chose to learn by being present with them in their world, where others were not present, and when others did not want to be present.

Jesus didn't want to let anything keep him away from learning, nor did he like the idea of postponing his service for some other time in order to be at the festival. He learned by being present in their world at the right time of their need, which was ignored by the Jewish world. Learning by detachment often omits the details and fails to understand the seriousness of an individual predicament. Lack of learning gives easy answers, while learning demands facing risk, asking tough questions, and avoiding the blame game. Jesus walked into the man's world to learn, not just accepting it as a necessary evil of society or limiting himself to learning by reading or hearing. His need to learn kept him away from the celebration of the Jewish feast and kept him in the place where he could bring hope and healing. To learn how the man felt when the rest of the society abandoned him, Jesus needed to abandon the feast and be present at Bethesda.

Jesus' learning came with a cost of being away from the feast; to know this man, his condition and his world was in stark contrast to the Jewish power structure and the feast at Jerusalem. His teaching attitude requires us to be humble, powerless and teachable. Learning comes with sacrifice; and learning about others comes at a steep price. Most of us learn to advance ourselves, upgrade our skills, and increase our competence and our market value, but Jesus brought a new understanding of learning for the sake of others. Such learning demands losing our self-interest and elevating others' interests. Such learning brings freedom for others and counters the unjust power structures and systems within society. Jesus empowers the weak and the marginalized, giving purpose, and establishing justice by becoming a learner near the pool. It is a courageous learning act that compels one to move into the space of those suffering and hurting fellow beings, and allows that environment to become part of the teaching process. Jesus allowed the weak of the society to teach the strong about how weak they really are. This reversal of educational approach was not normal and acceptable compared to the rigid, traditional system of the time.

Jesus demonstrated an act of learning on behalf of a man who was forgotten by the whole community. He learned by giving his time and attention to an individual who was forgotten by his own people, not just at any time but at the time of the feast. For Jesus, his feast would be incomplete until everyone was able to attend and be present at the table. Empty chairs at the family gathering compel Jesus to learn about those being ignored. He could not accept the religious power structure's exclusion of those who were weak from the celebration or from the family dinner due to prejudices and self-satisfying reasons. For him, no reason was good enough to allow the feast to continue without including those who were hurting and suffering at Bethesda.

When others decided to abide by the old rules taught by religion and society to accept the rejection of the disabled and weak of the society, Jesus moved to dismantle this discrimination. Just seeing one person being ignored or marginalized propelled him to act. He sought those who were distant, lost, and unaccounted for. He came to Bethesda to learn about the man, but taught a great deal to the whole of humanity by exposing our great ignorance, especially among the learned and religious people. A society that celebrates the festival while ignoring the weak, disabled and victims of injustice, and the families who keep silent or hide empty chairs is a society that has not learned the lesson of caring for needy people and thus participates in further promoting unfairness and injustice. The religious leaders who preached justice but promoted only the cause of the privileged class were in truth hurting humanity by carrying on evil practices.

2. Jesus learned about the mindset and the perspective behind the suffering. He learned the reason that kept the disabled from the feast, then he brought healing to the man and his community. Christ's visit to Bethesda at the time of the Jewish feast was not only to learn about a man who was disabled and cut off from his people but also to learn about the reason that kept him there. This need stretched Jesus to learn about his own Jewish people, their mindset, their worldview and their attitudes
toward their own, and about himself. His purpose was not to make himself self-aware or to advance his ideas or his

professional career, but rather to empower the weak and the marginalized and to help people learn the real purpose of the feast. Jesus' visit to Bethesda helps us redefine the true purpose of learning; unless the learning affects the lives of people and brings freedom or exposes our own blindness, our learning is self-serving and self-aggrandizing.

For Jesus, the life of this disabled man who was absent from the feast for thirty-eight years was something important for society to learn from and not something to shy away from or ignore. Any reason for society to ignore the weak and poor is too shallow to be accepted and each case too valuable to be ignored. It was not just about the man waiting at the pool for thirty-eight years, but about the society that for centuries had been disabled, paralyzed, blind, and poor toward its call, its real purpose and goals. The system and powers that kept the poor and needy hidden from the feast created a society that became oblivious to its vacuousness. This issue was significant enough and sufficient to attract learning.

Nothing short of an angelic intervention assured acceptance back into the community. Those who were first and fast, had help and were made whole—they were the ones who made it back into society. But many were left behind, those who were weak, had no resources, or were elderly. These are the ones who had no chance of making it back into society. There was no one to plead their case in the courts against the religious mafia and powerbrokers who deliberately wanted to ignore them, neglect them, and forget them, so they could benefit from their absence. The absence of some benefited the few.

Jesus did not ignore them, nor could he accept this culture's stance. He took time to learn about the man, to make him feel that he was not forgotten, to make him realize that he was cared for, that his empty chair at the feast was not a right and acceptable thing, and that someone did care for him. Jesus' learning was not based on mere mind expansion but involved a heart experience. The highest purpose of learning is to hear those who are never heard, see those who are invisible, and care for those who have been forgotten. For Jesus, the value behind such learning was not to make someone wealthy or rich, but to empty oneself to be near those who are poor and weak and make them rich by the presence of God and of caring people. This was a chance to extend that human dignity and value to the one who did not deserve it in the eyes of society— but in God's eyes he did.

Rabbi Jesus was required to learn about the religious requirements of the feast, but Jesus was careful to focus on a disabled, forgotten man at a stinky pool in the least-frequented neighborhood of Jerusalem. Jesus' passion to learn about this man during the feast shows a different attitude and character.

His learning exposed corruption. It exposed blindness. It exposed selfishness. Jesus exposed our hard hearts and our nature to ignore and to remain silent, and thus silently benefit from those who could not show up at the feast.

3. Jesus introduced learning to the feast to bring justice and wholeness to the community. Christ's learning about the man who had been in his condition for a long time compelled him to do something more than just physically heal him. Jesus brought mercy and justice into the celebration of the feast. After his visit to Bethesda, the feast was looked upon with fresh eyes. Jesus wanted the learning to result in freedom, justice, and mercy for the oppressed in society. His learning challenged the powers that be. He wanted this newfound wisdom to result in valuing every human life and respecting each person as being created in the image of God.

Jesus was very deliberate in making his intentions clear by visiting Bethesda at that time of the year and seeing the man, learning about him and his condition so that he could show the world what God truly desires in such a situation. When most of learning at that time revolved around the interpretation of the laws and the way to manipulate God's voice for human gain, Jesus set the true learners and seekers free by showing them a new approach and reason for learning. He also courageously proclaimed that learning need not be for greed or ego or self-interest, but it can become a tool to free humans from the clutches of evil masters who are the product of wrong learning. True learning can bring healing, mercy, and justice to humanity. It can give people new joy to learn and make changes that affect the community in a profound and positive way.

The Dark Streets of Mumbai. To be a voice for the voiceless and those forgotten, for invisible and unaccounted for children can be a real challenge at times. But that is exactly what Prakash found himself surrounded by when he arrived for his new assignment as the director for a non-governmental organization (NGO) involved in rescuing girls who were trapped in human trafficking in Mumbai, India.

I have known Prakash for several years, and I knew he wanted to bring hope and encouragement to those who never had the opportunity to receive it. His life overflows with compassion. Growing up in one of the poor rural parts of India, he had experienced loss, rejection, and poverty firsthand. He lived in an unhappy home with an alcoholic father who was mostly absent and lost his mother at a very young age. All of these negative factors affected him deeply and led him into a state of depression. Seeing no future, he resigned himself to just exist and spend the rest of his life with no purpose.

Then one day, a young man came to Prakash's village and attempted to become his friend; and over the next several visits, he introduced Prakash, for the first time, to the good news of the Savior, one who could change his life, a God who was there for him, who promised a future of life here and now and and hereafter. Prakash came to know in a very personal way about the one who was willing to meet him right where he was in his life—when he was hopeless, depressed, and in his own Bethesda. Prakash was filled with hope because there was nothing for him to lose and nothing else to hope for. He soon embarked on a new life and an altogether new and exciting journey. He studied hard and bonded with a few people who had shown light into his life and had for the first time given him hope.

In his own words, "I started living once again, it was a new voice to my dead self." Prakash, in the following years, developed into a fine young man, dedicated and passionate and committed to his faith in the one who changed him by living in him. Then he had a breakthrough; he was hired to be part of a growing community development agency and soon learned the art of administration and business. This was the experience that brought him to his new position in the city; a city which has a dark and dangerous face at night.

Prakash quickly found the work not only rewarding but also very challenging as he had to negotiate with dishonest officials who had made deals with the power mongers of the dark world. The more he faced opposition, the more he found reason to be energized to move forward and make every effort to rescue the helpless children who were being abducted and sold as sex-slaves to satisfy the perverted appetites of the rich and famous of the city. He knew his fight was not against *flesh and blood* but against the *principalities* and darkness that controlled the atmosphere (see Ephesians 6:12).

Prakash encouraged his friends to be more aggressive in praying for the rescue operation. They joined together and also received favor from the police force of the city. With all the help he could get, he started moving into the streets, the neighborhoods where these young girls were kept captive. Slowly he found light shining into these dark corners and felt God breaking in and pushing him forward in his work in setting the prisoners free.

During one of his interviews with the media, Prakash could not hold back his tears when he described how many of the young girls where hidden and trapped in between closed walls by the pimps who kept them out of sight from the police. They were only taken outside to be used multiple times by their slave traders to make themselves rich by sacrificing these innocent lives. At the end, Prakash mentioned that the greatest gift he could ever give to these precious girls was to bring a smile back to their faces—the sweet faces of forgotten, unaccounted for, invisible yet beautiful little girls. After being freed and living a different life surrounded by the love of the caring rescue workers, one of the girls said, with tears of joy in her eyes, "This is the first time…I feel I am alive."

Though the emotional and physical trauma and scars left behind by the perpetrators are very deep and real and the girls will need long-term help, therapy and maybe many years to heal, they are now free—free to live, free to once again dream, and free to proclaim that God's light shines even in the darkest places. What a story of redemption that started with one life dedicated for God's mission and his glory that went on to set others free!

***

That story was fresh in my mind while sitting with a group of offenders who were part of the sex-offenders rehabilitation program. Rescuing poor, innocent girls from evil hands is very important but just leaving the offender behind bars is not enough. Restorative justice compels us to reach out to remove the perverted thinking patterns that give birth to such heinous behaviors. It is a hard task and one of the ways the group leader was helping these young inmates was to look within them by asking questions. Questions that move beyond the surface and look deeper within themselves and their community to hear what they have never heard before. To once again listen to the voice that they had killed many times before they ever committed any crime.

Jesus Asked

One man at Bethesda had been an invalid for thirty-eight years. When Jesus saw him lying there and learned that he had been in this condition for a long time, he asked the man, "Do you want to get well?" A question that was probably never asked before.

Jesus went to Bethesda during the feast of the Jews, saw a man, learned about his condition, and then *asked* the man a question. He did not preach or teach (although he was the greatest teacher and preacher), He did not blame or rebuke, He *asked*. Asking gives others a chance to express themselves, gives others a feeling of being heard, and ultimately empowers others. Jesus did this at Bethesda. He gave the man a voice, a place to speak, and time to listen to him. Jesus came to Bethesda to learn what others did not know about the man, to get to know him, and ask how he was different from how he was perceived to be. Jesus *asked* a question that empowered the ordinary, disabled, forgotten citizens of Jewish society. Jesus asked for three reasons: 1) to give voice to the voiceless, forgotten people of Bethesda; 2) to give voice to the inner man of the disabled man rather than his circumstance or situation;

and 3) to give voice to God's plan, purpose, and power and the dream he had planted in this man.

The way of Jesus at the pool of Bethesda was revolutionary. He did not come as a savior (although he is the only one who can save humanity from its sin) who did not care about others' thoughts, he came as someone who wanted to genuinely know what the poor, needy, disabled, and forgotten were feeling. Jesus wanted the world to understand the man from his place, see him from his vantage point. For the first time, people would hear from the one who was lying at the pool, from his perspective, not from what was thrust upon him by the outside world. Jesus gave an opportunity for his story to be shared with the world. Jesus wanted to acknowledge the importance and value of his inside world that was shut out for so long, and for that reason Jesus entered into the hidden world of Bethesda. This was the same reason Jesus came to his own, and the same reason the Father gave his only begotten son! (See John 3:16-17.)

1. *Jesus asked...to give voice to the voiceless, forgotten people of Bethesda.* Jesus walked to the man who was disabled and ignored and asked him an important question. Many had written him off, considered him unqualified to speak up for himself, or didn't think he had anything of worth to say. Many very well-qualified leaders had supplied various "right" reasons

to explain his condition. Many might have thought him to be a burden to the state, but may never have taken the time to understand him by giving him a voice. There were many others who fell in the same category as this man, and society was always prepared to ship them to a place of no return. But Jesus walked into that suppressed and silenced place, and turned up the volume and gave the man a voice.

Jesus made sure that people understood that this forgotten man's voice was important and that he believed in what the man had to say. He testified that there is truth to his story even though it was never heard before. Jesus gave ear to the voices buried under the weight of religious burden and rigid tradition. The way of grace gave strength to the weak to speak up in freedom, boldness and honesty about how they truly felt inside. By his visit to Bethesda, Jesus paused the feast so that the crowd would listen to what this man who was forgotten for thirty-eight years had to say. The resurrection of the man's lost voice was the first miracle on his path toward physical healing; it was the healing of his soul. The voice that was suppressed unless an angelic stirring allowed it, was suddenly heard loud and clear because of a bigger stirring caused by the silencing of the lamb of God, the savior of humankind on the cross of Calvary.

2. *Jesus asked…to give voice to the man's inner self* *and not his circumstance or situation.* The man at the pool of Bethesda had been there for a long time. He had seen, heard, and experienced many things over the past thirty-eight years. Since the day he arrived at the pool, the hope of getting well and returning back to society and of being reunited with his loved ones had changed. After seeing the daily hopelessness around him and experiencing it personally, the constant reminder of an already failed life left him defeated.

Slowly the man withdrew himself into the painful reality of his surroundings. The difficult sight of watching others walk out of the water with their healing and repeatedly being left out and missing the miracle made him a changed man, a man with a new voice and that suppressed the original voice deep within that longed to be set free against all odds. That faint small voice still believed he could be part of the feast and hoped that maybe one day someone would take pity on him and carry him into the water as soon as it was stirred. But that voice had faltered.

To his surprise, he found many within his new community who believed as he did in the initial days but now had given up hope. The inner voice of this man struggled to find even a single soul for comfort and support. There were no words of encouragement and faith uttered, and under such famished conditions his voice fell silent, almost as if it never existed. Often under the heavy weight of crime, guilt and shame, one's true inner voice dies.

> *When Jesus saw him lying there and learned that he*
> *had been in this condition for a long time, he asked him,*
> **"Do you want to get well?"** (John 5:6 NIV).

Jesus steps onto the covered porches of Bethesda and sees the man, learns about him, and asks him the question, "Do you want to get well?" Jesus asks the inner man to speak up and to take back his right once again to make his voice heard.

> *"Sir," the invalid replied, "I have no one to help me*
> *into the pool when the water is stirred. While I am*
> *trying to get in, someone else goes down ahead of me"*
> (John 5:7 NIV).

Jesus' purpose was to make the inner voice heard and to allow that feeble voice that had been suppressed for the past thirty-eight years to speak up once again. This would give the man the strength to believe that everything is possible for those who believe (see Mark 9:23). Jesus appeared at the Bethesda pool not only to give voice to the disabled and forgotten but to call every person to believe in the bigger and greater purposes of God. That voice tells us that situations and circumstances do not define who we are—rather, the promises and purposes of God dictate and shape our lives. The prophet of old rightly predicted of this Messiah (Isaiah 42:3-4 NIV), "A bruised reed he will not break, and a smoldering wick he will not snuff out. In faithfulness he will bring forth justice; he will not falter or be discouraged till he establishes justice on earth. In his teaching the islands will put their hope." We say amen! Jesus came to bring justice to humanity by healing the oppressed soul by giving back his rightful voice.

3. *Jesus asked...to give a voice to God's plan, purpose, and his power.* Jesus came to express to the broken and defeated person that God has a plan and purpose, and his power is available even during the darkest and hardest moments of life. The man who was forgotten and erased from the memories of his friends and family and people at the feast had to be made known as an example that God never forgets and he never ignores us when we are weak and defeated. God comes and meets us and tells us that he has a plan and a purpose for our lives—and the power is available for us to see things in a different light even when others don't believe in us or even when we don't trust ourselves.

Jesus asked the man, "Do you want to get well?" so that the man would know there was more to his life and purpose than what society and his condition had determined. Jesus asked the important question so that the power of God would be made known. Over and above all the sickness, disease, and even failure and rejection, Jesus has the authority to ask him— and us, "Do you want to get well?"

In the next chapter we will see some deeper issues surfacing as this question echoes in Bethesda and beyond.

Questions to Ponder

*When Jesus saw him lying there and **learned** that he had been in this condition for a long time, he asked him, "Do you want to get well?" (John 5:6 NIV).*

1. Jesus learned by <u>entering</u> the disabled man's world.

   Do we enter others' worlds to learn about them? What are the ways we learn about others?

2. Jesus learned about the <u>mindset</u> and the perspective behind the suffering. He learned the <u>reason</u> that kept the disabled from the feast.

   What are some mindsets or reasons behind human suffering and marginalization in our community?

3. Jesus <u>introduced learning</u> to the feast to bring justice and wholeness to the community.

   How is learning important for holistic ministry?

4. Jesus asked a question to give <u>voice</u> to the <u>forgotten people</u> of Bethesda.

   Whose voices have we failed to hear and why?

5. Jesus asked to give <u>voice</u> to the <u>man's inner self</u> and not his circumstance or situation.

   Is there a voice within us or in others that has never been heard?

6. Jesus asked to give voice to God's plan, purpose, and his power.

Do we hear God's voice over our circumstances? If so how is it different?

CHAPTER FIVE

THE UNSETTLING QUESTION

We may speak about a place where there are no tears, no death, no fear, no night; but those are just the benefits of heaven. The beauty of heaven is seeing God. –Max Lucado

I wasn't paying attention as Martha walked hurriedly past by my office. Usually I make it a point to meet the people who come to speak at the chapel. But that evening I just missed it. We had a special class where victims of crime are invited to share their story to help offenders understand the cost of crime, and how it imprisons the family, especially children that live with shame, and cripples the whole community. I got to officially meet Martha when she was introduced on stage. She began speaking to a room full of male offenders. She didn't sugarcoat her words. She was blunt and detailed in describing what happened to her fifteen years ago and how it totally changed her, her family and her world.

She was intense and careful in reporting everything that occurred to her on that horrific night when she was brutally raped multiple times by a man at knifepoint. She had just hung up the phone after a call from her mother to confirm plans to spend time together for the upcoming Mother's Day. Martha worked as a nurse's assistant in a small clinic in the remote part of the city that staffed a maximum of five people on a busy day including the part-time doctors. That evening, mostly everyone had already left for the day. Martha was preparing to close the office when the man quietly entered. Initially it looked like he was there for a delivery, but within no time he locked the door behind her and without losing a moment pointed his knife and ordered her to move into the back room. There he inhumanely assaulted her sexually and left her in a semi-unconscious state before walking out into the darkness. Martha was badly wounded, in shock, fear and in tremendous pain as she regained her

consciousness. She didn't know if she would ever gain the strength to lift herself up from the ground. But somehow she managed to crawl to the phone and called the police. Soon the paramedics also arrived and she was shifted to the emergency care in the nearby hospital. It was just the beginning of the ordeal that Martha had to live through for the next seven very difficult years. The first few weeks were spent in intensive care where she battled for her very life. Though her life was spared, that night changed everything about her. She wasn't the same person anymore. According to her family, it felt like they lost their child after that gruesome incident. Though the man was arrested and sentenced to prison, Martha's life went downhill from that point forward. She lost her job, she underwent many court proceedings where she had to face various investigations and trials causing intense emotional trauma. All of it stressed her greatly, and to lessen the pain, she started drinking heavily, overmedicating herself and living a life on the edge. She had attempted to kill herself twice to escape from the terrible bouts of depression and trauma. She hated men and crowds and usually confined herself within the dark walls of her one-room apartment. She often lived on welfare and barely managed to keep a steady job.

Sitting there among the crowd and listening to the tragic effects of crime on innocent lives, I shuddered with fear and anger. What took the audience that night by surprise was her describing the journey of meeting with her attacker in the prison a few years later. She wanted to find out why he did what he did and why he chose to destroy a life. She wanted to let him know that his actions had permanently damaged her life as well as many others' lives. She said the night before she was going to meet her attacker, she couldn't sleep. To find some peace, she tried to spend some time in silence and prayer, but it was a struggle.

But at midnight something happened. A strength came over her and she experienced a peace that allowed her to escape the mental prison she was living in because of the tragedy. All the anger and pain she was harboring inside her had been suffocating her. But in that moment she decided to let go and forgive the person who had committed the horrendous crime against her. She said in a soft but firm voice, "That night, I felt a new person living within me as I decided that I would not allow this man to hurt me anymore and cage me any longer. I am going to release myself from this suffering by forgiving him." There was pin-drop silence all around in the chapel. No one moved or said anything except those trying to wipe away tears with their tattooed hands. Tears were rolling down from the rough cheeks of some hardened offenders for the very first time. Before she left the room, she looked once again into their eyes and said, "I never knew there was an option to get well before that

night." Her story is the story of many victims whose lives have changed forever at the hands of evildoers. But that night a different message echoed within the prison walls of Estelle:

The power of redemption and forgiveness can set any captive free.

***

During the feast of the Jews, Jesus arrives at Bethesda and sees a man and learns that he has been in that condition of sickness for a long time and then asks him a personal, simple yet powerful question: "Do you want to get well?"

It seems to be a simple or rather unqualified or unnecessary question to ask a man who has been sick for more than three decades in an environment not very conducive to a normal standard of living. It is like asking a patient in the hospital if he really needs medical treatment to get well. But examined within the context of the larger picture of what this man represents and what his situation signifies, it truly calls for deeper investigation.

Jesus asks a very direct question that addresses the following three key aspects of this man lying near the pool of Bethesda for thirty-eight years:

1. **Compromise**: The man's life of sickness, failure, being marginalized and forgotten devalued his sense of worth, made him blind to any option of healing, and caused him to settle for a lower, substandard lifestyle due to a confused identity.

2. **Oppression**: The man at the pool represented a large segment of the society that was unaccounted for during the most important festive time of the Jews. His desire to get well would require the healing of a society that was oppressive to its own people and caused many to disappear from the feast.

3. **Mission**: The man's healing spoke of God, his power, his compassion, his ways, and his mission to the broken world. A mission through which God still speaks to the broken world to show his power and his glory and confirm that he is still at work and in control.

Bethesda attracted people who were filled with agony and suffering; they did not fit into "normal" Jewish society. People who were not needed or wanted by society went to Bethesda with a hope—a hope of healing, new life, and a better way of life. They soon discovered that the place had nothing more to offer than hopelessness, failure, and further rejection.

Failing in Jerusalem gave people an option to run to Bethesda; but what do they do when they fail in Bethesda? Where can they run from there? Time after time they miss the opportunity of healing when the water is stirred because others were faster or had help, and thus entered the water before them. Bethesda becomes a place of intense suffering for those who are left out and couldn't afford the resources or help. Although they entered the water only seconds later than others, the opportunity for healing just vanished—just like that, and along with it their hope.

It is easy for people in that suffering community to complain, get depressed and discouraged. That is when Jesus walks in and meets the man who was in that camp of people for so long and had hoped against hope until one day hope itself died. After the death of hope, each new day meant a life of compromise, an abnormal life, and a losing battle, allowing the oppression of mainstream society to continue unchecked, and giving no place for God's mission or work to happen.

Let us examine each of these points in greater detail.

1. Compromise. *The man's life of sickness, failure, being marginalized and forgotten devalued his sense of worth, made him blind to the option of healing, and caused him to settle for a lower, compromised lifestyle.* Repeated failure can alter or diminish the value of success and one's own worth. Few people are able to distance themselves from such repeated tragedy, failure, abuse, or hurt, scrape out that little bit of strength, and rise up. Being down for a long time is hard, frightening, shameful, and often lonely. Expecting a comeback is hard and often next to impossible. Most people often give up fighting or do not even try to rise again when they have failed in such a hard way—and even rarer still if they have failed repeatedly. The once coveted dream of theirs is shattered, their hope of getting well or being stable is crushed, as they keep failing again and again. Then there comes a point when things change. Change that is not for the better. Change that alters the outlook, expectations and forces a new future that is defined and determined by compromise.

When this happens, most of us are forced to find other things to do, forgetting the past and moving on to find a different meaning and purpose in something else or usually settling for a compromised lifestyle. In the process, we unknowingly lower the bar, our dreams die, relational expectations are minimal, and we live a life of compromise. For some it may hurt for a while initially and may make them discouraged when they see others still going after their dreams and living a life they once wished they could live.

Let's make this situation personal: Perhaps seeing those coming out of the pool healed and watching them collect their belongings and emptying their living quarters, makes you think, *Why did I ever give up on my dreams?* The dream of getting whole again brought you to Bethesda. But now after being here for too long and experiencing all those failures, the dream—the very reason for being at Bethesda—has become too painful, difficult, and too personal—you do not even want to remember it or mention it. The suffering that Bethesda offers due to the compromised life, when compared to the pain of keeping the original dream alive, is more tolerable. Hence you opt for it and purchase it as a way to calm yourself.

Occasionally your circumstances due to this compromise can cause mild depression or maybe a few bouts of insomnia, making you wake up in the middle of the night with those suppressed dreams flashing in your mind, accompanied with some cold sweats. Those rare nightmares may force you to think about what your life would have been or what you could have achieved if those dreams were not buried alive, or if you were still pursuing them. But as time goes by those thoughts fade or get less intense. You may pop some pills to get over it. Moreover, those in your adopted family of sufferers (your company in Bethesda), who also are facing the similar agony of lost dreams, come to your rescue, they surround you and offer comfort. Soon you find solace in that clique. And your dream is put on the backburner never to see the spark of fire again.

Though it is said that in the company of other sufferers pain is reduced, in reality there comes a time when each of us finds ourselves all alone and afraid. Then we face the *dark night of the soul*. We shed tears that soak our pillows, and sleep late into the day. The comfort of our friends in those moments of heartache helps a little, but often it is very hard to describe or even share our deep struggles with them because each of us experiences pain very differently. Although we know deep in our own hearts that this kind of group is not a true shield from our inner turmoil, yet for the sake of false hope, we hold onto it and keep them close. They are the only ones we have left when others rejected us. For some, they have been driven out from their neighborhood, others have had eviction notices posted on their front doors so that everyone including their children's friends and families know they had fallen behind in mortgage payments. Every compromised life has a story, and a painful one.

Dream a Dream: Whether you chose to take the hard road or you woke up one day and found yourself there, falling in with the company of such a group (compromisers) only helps momentarily. But these "friends" also frequently destroy the strength you need to dream again. Even if you indulge yourself in nostalgia, remembering your old dream of getting a new job, restoring important relationships, or going back to school, your friends may feel threatened and may determine to squash your true, inner self's desires, your dream. They may see your dream as a betrayal.

Soon your dream becomes the center of a battle between the outside world and the inside self. You not only fight against your inner desires but may even seek help from your friends to provide that support and strength to fight against what you know deep down is God's will. While you are fighting this battle, the feast on the streets of old Jerusalem is at a fever pitch. Some are happy that you are gone and that you have found new friends near the pool. As long as you are cared for by these friends and they keep you lured away, then your chair remains empty. They selfishly want you to stay away. That way they can enjoy what rightfully belongs to you.

Bethesda becomes a strange place, the water that once attracted you to it now repels you. You cannot hide from it, nor can you behold it. That is the story for many until they see the sight of the one thirsting and dying on the cross to offer that fresh living water to everyone who comes to him.

Jesus walks into Bethesda with full knowledge of the man's compromised life. He also knew what was holding this man—and what is holding us—and how his absence wrongfully benefited a few at the feast, and how it no longer bothered him. With this knowledge Jesus asks him—and us—the question, "Do you want to get well?"

Rick's Story

I found Rick when he was near his so-called Bethesda. Those who had known him in his previous life (before he became part of the newfound group he called his buddies), often fail to recognize him in his new avatar, his new identity. Rick grew up in an upscale urban neighborhood and attended a private school where he was part of the gifted and talented student program. According to him, everything was going fine until he and a few of his classmates were accidentally exposed to pornography. For others it was just a passing phase, but for Rick it was something that gripped him and became impossible to shake. It was a fantasy that seemed to offer him escape.

He quickly became hooked. For hours and sometimes all night he would surf adult sites in the privacy of his room. Initially he tried to get out of it, but failed as he didn't have the courage to ask for help because he felt ashamed. His addiction caused him to feel hopeless. None of his family members were aware of the secret he was hiding. He was able to manage his academic life, which meant everything to his family. And so he carried this addiction into adulthood. He married an attractive dentist, whom he met at one of his best friend's weddings. He worked for a healthcare firm that gave him a decent living. A few years into their marriage, the couple was making plans to adopt a little girl.

Just when he thought everything was going right, without warning the demon from his past raised its ugly head, manifesting in various forms. Rick did not realize how bad things were and the depth of his entangled addiction. Some days he fought depression with suicidal thoughts, sometimes he was not able to control his anger, other days he arrived late to work and on a few occasions, he never showed up at all. Having no valid excuse for such behaviors, he was confronted by his wife several times to seek help, and she made several attempts to schedule him for professional counseling, but nothing worked as a lasting remedy. She did suspect early on that something was odd in the relationship, but she could not put her finger on anything specific.

Rick had mastered the art of deception. The darkness within him had overpowered him and he had become a slave to sex and pornography. The addiction had not only caused his career downfall, he was also at the point of losing his family. Rick had become a different person, hanging out with a different group of friends and spending most of his days and nights with them. They were totally engrossed in deep sexual addiction, games, and fantasies, as well as highly involved with drugs. To feed his addictive behavior, he had to cheat, steal and borrow money from various sources which now meant he had another problem—a problem with the law.

So when I met Rick, I felt deeply sorry for him and for his family because of what his addiction had caused. Yet none of it bothered Rick as he was not able to see the hurt and the suffering his family was going through. His only concern was about not losing his so-called buddies who were supporting and encouraging his addictive habit. He could not see what all he was giving up to support this destructive lifestyle. He was almost at the point of no return because he did not believe that he could come out of his condition. He thought he didn't have the strength to fight his addiction and so found this state to be his new home, his living and his purpose. Everything else, even his wife and family were seen as distracting him from his pleasurable new way of life.

For him, the "poolside friends" (as it was for the man at Bethesda) were better than his true and meaningful family relationships. He had tried fighting the battle for a long time and lost, and now he didn't have the strength to fight anymore. The only fight he fought was with those who wanted him to battle his addiction. His dreams, his wife's dreams, and the dreams they shared together were sacrificed on the altar of pornography, sexual pleasure, a perverted lifestyle, and the friends he surrounded himself with. They prevented him from ever dreaming of a normal life again.

The man at Bethesda had been sick for a long time—too long for anyone to hope for or even expect something new or different to happen. He was discouraged, abandoned, and tasted the pain of failure so many times that he had lost interest in being healed. He accepted sickness as normal and stopped trying to get healed, stopped fighting against the Jewish society that had marginalized and ignored him at the festival. Rather, he was now fighting the second marginalization experienced in Bethesda from those who were being healed. Being among the less fortunate who were never helped and had no chance to step into the water at the right time to claim their healing had pushed him into a second rejection.

There was no place he could go from here. So he compromised and accepted this as his new home and found new ways to become "normal" again. And that is when Jesus came and asked him a question that burst the bubble that he was living in. It would disrupt his comfort and disturb his last place of refuge. He had distanced himself so far from the real world that even the prospect of being healed caused him fear. He had been at Bethesda for so long that a new option was a threat. He was like a traveler who had gone to a distant land to do business, to make a living for his family back home, but then abandoned everything at home, and slowly settled into his new place. With a newfound company of sick and diseased friends, he started making this transient place his final destination.

Jesus selected him as the man to talk to on this most auspicious festive day on the Jewish calendar and asks him a challenging question, "Do you want to get well?"

For this man, getting well-meant three things:

1) Giving up his new friends, the ones who are traveling in the same boat with him, the company of failures and compromisers;

2) Giving up the minor victories he came to depend on such as collecting and selling things like belongings and toys left behind by those who were healed and left Bethesda; and

3) Dreaming again, risking again, believing again, hoping again, and above all having faith again.

2. Oppression. *The man at the pool represented a large segment of society that was unaccounted for during the most important festive time of the Jews. His desire to get well required the healing of a society that was oppressive to its own people and was the reason for the disappearance of many from the feast.* Jesus not only learned about the condition of the man at the Bethesda pool but also exposed deep-rooted corruption in that society. How could they be so harsh and insensitive to the needs of their own people during their annual feast?

Jesus asked the man, "Do you want to get well?" It was also a question to the larger Jewish religious establishment and to every oppressive society that had victimized its people and deprived them of their God-given dignity. This question exposed their hardened, corrupt human hearts. It showed how we oppress our own and how we gain from others' pain.

How have we become people so ignorant and insensitive in the name of religion? Even during religious celebrations we shut out our own people and don't feel any guilt or shame about it. We don't have the answers to those difficult questions that surround us—and many times we do not even ask any questions at all. We frequently tend to find excuses and blame the situation. We may offer a little sympathy, but we are not aware of the deep sickness within our society. We are crafty in hiding those who have left empty chairs behind—making them visible only on the pages of some NGO's fundraising brochures. Marginalized and oppressed people of our society who have been abandoned, neglected, and forgotten are not even an issue during the feast. The worst thing that has happened to us is that we do not see it as an evil practice or as a disease affecting society.

Unless we are aware of our sickness, we do not seek a healer. Therefore, Jesus coming to Bethesda during the feast of the Jews highlighted to everyone who could hear—and did not want to hear—that there was an abysmal deep-rooted sickness that afflicted the human heart and had spread into the community and into our worship as well as in our celebrations. We have lived in that guilt for so long that we don't even acknowledge it or take responsibility for our part. But sadly it won't go away. People are still suffering because of an uncaring attitude by individuals and communities and nations as a whole. So this question strikes at the center of our faith, family, and community, "Do you want to get well?" Are we willing to make room for the healing? Would we be willing to make some changes in our behavior/attitude to accommodate those we have forgotten in our busyness of celebrating the feast? Would we be willing to dust off those old chairs that have been empty for years and welcome the lost and lonely back into our midst?

Would we make room in our hearts first for those who are weak and poor and those who are not able to provide for themselves? Here the healing is important—but the change in lifestyle that healing demands is what causes the stirring, the true stirring of many souls. The man at the pool, the Jewish community, and every human heart, make excuses and do not immediately accept healing because doing so would be to acknowledge our true failure and pathetic condition. It is easier to find an excuse than to be real and seek healing.

Accepting healing would affect many who want to make their living off the sufferers, as well as derive false identity from the sickness. According to them they are the "good, religious people," who are carrying out the religious works all in the name of religion. Yet they become stumbling blocks to the very work of God. They even promote indifference in the treatment of those who are suffering so that Bethesda remains populated as well as segregated and they can maintain their good posture and position in life.

Jesus' question to an invalid man at the pool of Bethesda disturbed religious, political, financial, and every sector that finds its purpose and meaning in creating an identity by ignoring the suffering of those less fortunate and the innocent voiceless children of God. There are many who come with superficial solutions to make them look good in front of others. They are not willing to acknowledge that they are the ones who are sick, but Jesus knew how deep the disease had spread and how people had completely ignored the truth and accepted the falsehood.

Some of our religious activities break the heart of God. Today our community has failed to see the widespread disease that has crippled our young and ambitious generation by causing them to believe that all that is needed is the right appearance and image, to look good even when there are wounds and sickness within us. Jesus comes knocking at the door of our religious, financial, and political systems and asks if anyone is willing to open the door and allow the Great Physician to come in. Are we willing to accept the reality of our condition and acknowledge our need of the Savior and make room for the change required in our hearts and minds?

Do we want to get healed? Healed of our selfishness, insensitivity, indifference, and silence when people around us are suffering, marginalized, and absent from experiencing life, joy, and hope. Do we as a society care enough to be healed by campaigning against the wrong practices and the frauds within our society that in the name of positional leadership are wolves in sheep's clothing, hurting the innocent and weak ones in society? Do we want to be healed to become a people who are able to accept, include, and celebrate differences and weaknesses in others? On the day of the great feast of the Jews, Jesus walked away from Jerusalem and stood near the pool of

Bethesda. In the same way he walked from heaven and came into our world and is still asking each of us today, "Do you want to be healed?"

3. Mission. *The man's healing spoke of God, his power, his compassion, his ways, and his mission to the broken world.* "Do you want to get well?" A question that can push us to a place where we will have to lift both our hands in surrender and give up control. And that is when the power of God is released, experienced and understood, when weakness celebrates God's strength and compassion, and when humility embraces the work of God. Jesus comes to the forgotten place of Bethesda and shows that God's heart is moved to go where others fail or refuse to go. It also shows that God is still active and able to work beyond our usual expectations and our limitations, healing us even when the water is not stirred.

Healing is also for those who are not fast or favored. It is also for the forgotten and for those who always end up last and have been stuck in one place for a long time. There is hope for those who have faced mighty waves of tragedies and are on the verge of giving up. The visit of Jesus to Bethesda opened the eyes of the people who thought the mission of healing was meant only for the disabled, lame, and paralyzed, but never thought that it was the religious structure that was lame, blind, and paralyzed. It opened a new way of allowing God to work and heal and restore, beyond religious norms and traditions. For the first time, it allowed people in Bethesda to seek healing beyond what they had experienced and to allow the greater work of God to flow freely. It attracted and inspired a new generation of worshipers who were not content with rituals and routines, but were captured by his Spirit and truth. They were the ones who were willing to pour the new wine in the new wineskins to witness a fresh anointing of God beyond every human idea, plan and work.

Once again the power of God was allowed to move freely beyond the mindset of certain patterns. Jesus, with his visit to Bethesda, triggered a new tradition where people didn't have to limit God to human parameters. For the first time people were open to seeking healing beyond the stirred water. They realized that God's mission was about proclaiming his work, in his way—and his mercy was for everyone who was willing and waiting.

Questions to Ponder

"Do you want to get well?" (John 5:6 NIV).

1. Do you see any compromise in your life due to any reason that has caused you to settle for less?

2. Are others' healings dependent on your healing? Where is the healing needed in your life so that others may get their healing?

3. If Jesus asks you, "Do you want to get well?" what would be your answer?

CHAPTER SIX

THE MAN AND THE MIRACLE

He said "Love...as I have loved you." We cannot love too much.

—Amy Carmichael

"Sir," the invalid replied, "I have no one to help me into the pool when the water is stirred. While I am trying to get in, someone else goes down ahead of me." **Then Jesus said to him, "Get up! Pick up your mat and walk."** *At once the man was cured;* *he picked up his mat and walked. The day on which this took place was a Sabbath, and so the Jewish leaders said to the man who had been healed, "It is the Sabbath; the law forbids you to carry your mat." But*

he replied, "The man who made me well said to me,
'Pick up your mat and walk.'" So they asked him,
"Who is this fellow who told you to pick it up and
walk?" The man who was healed had no idea who it
was, for Jesus had slipped away into the crowd that was
there (John 5:7-13 NIV).

Jesus saw, learned, and asked an important question to the invalid man at the pool of Bethesda, who was lying there for thirty-eight years. The man's reply provided detailed facts about him and his situation, but lacked the understanding of who God is and what he can do. Deleting God for any reason or under any pressure promotes a lifestyle of compromise because it kills the hope that only God can bring. Even though he was a Jew, he was separated from the Jewish experience of the feast and what it could offer him; similarly, he must have thought he was separated from God and what he could offer him. Being in Bethesda in such a condition for so long, the man's reply focused on his past and his present, and predicted a hopeless future unless something supernatural happened to him. After thirty-eight long years, he thought he would remain in the same situation until he died. He accepted the facts and it shaped his future, but there is more to life than just facts as we humans understand it. Faith allows one to rise above and reach a place where facts fall short and fail, but hope stands strong and miracles are seen.

The man's life experience and situation took him to a place where failure did not scare him anymore, nor did the prospect of a better future excite him. A life of compromise was defining a new meaning, identity and providing a community which he did not wish to give up on or trade for anything. The only way Jesus could speak to the man's spirit (the toil experienced by his body had slowly crippled him inside), was to connect with his inner self. He had to appear to the nearly dying inner spirit as the one who held the authority over life and death, the one who had the power to call the dead to breathe again and command Lazarus to leave the tomb and walk out.

Therefore, Jesus *commands* the man to first *"Get up!"* then *"Pick up,"* and *"Walk."* These three commands each have their own significance for the man, his life, and his future. We shall look into each one to understand the man and the miracle.

Get Up. Jesus' presence at the pool of Bethesda introduced a new way for the work of God and the power of God. He was there to resurrect that which was diseased, destroyed, and deliberately diminished, which otherwise could have been touching a new destiny, taking a new direction, with new determination. Jesus is not at all denying the hard facts faced by the man or devaluing his statements, rather he was inviting the invalid into a miracle that wasn't just for the fast or the first. Healing that is not refused due to our weakness and lack of resources—but a miracle that totally dependent on God's grace and his power.

This new miraculous way moves beyond human tradition, ideas, comprehension, and can rescue us from every power within humanity, the world and beyond. Jesus did not then and does not now fail to help those who have developed a compromised lifestyle due to the disadvantages and oppression they have faced by the community or society because of the burden of our sin, guilt and shame. Jesus walked into Bethesda to restore the man, the system, the community—and above all to inaugurate a new understanding of God to the broken world. By commanding the man to get up, Jesus was breathing the Spirit back into the man—and his community.

For a man who had been lying down for so long, getting up does not come so easily. There is no strength or voice that is able to speak from within to cause him to rise. Everything that he heard repeatedly spoken over and over for thirty-eight years was to lie there, give up, and accept his fate. In the natural, perhaps the man thought that the words Jesus uttered for him to get up were not meant for him,. Perhaps he didn't feel qualified to receive a command to get up. Maybe the command made him think he wasn't worthy to even entertain the idea that these words were meant for him. It would have been easy and normal for him to have accepted the lying down part, but Jesus' words gave him the option for the first time in many years to briefly dream of being accidentally qualified for such a command.

Moses the leader and the deliverer of Israelites experienced a similar dilemma when confronted by the Almighty. God asked him to go back to Egypt to set the Israelites free and Moses thought he didn't fit the bill. He thought God would be better off if he chose someone other than a murderer, stutterer and fugitive. But God wanted him to get up, pick up and walk as he led him. God is the same today as he was then.

Making it Personal

It is one thing to be qualified for healing, but it is entirely another thing to accept it and make it personal. Those words—*get up*—were never spoken to him by anyone, because his situation disqualified him from meriting such favor. Aware of his prolonged wait for healing, people would choose words that were crumbs to sustain him, but they would never offer such hope as to say get up. Coming from them those would be empty words, false promises or even an ethical violation because the protocol was that the water had to be stirred first before healing could come. Asking the man to get up was to toy with the emotions of an already hurting man.

But Jesus appears on the scene with authority and mercy. He meets the man without any blinders, removes every barrier, and brings him to a place where the man was equally worthy to hear the words "Get up." Jesus told him to get up even when the world was against him, to get up even when the angels had failed him, to get up even when it had been ages since he ever stood on his own two feet, get up when he was still the last, get up even when there was no one to help him and to get up even when he didn't see healing as a possibility. For the first time in thirty-eight years there was a *get up* option to choose. And there was no guilt about it.

For Jesus, the man's past, his present, other people's ideas, and other powers did not define what rightfully belonged to the man—what the man could claim by answering his question. This person's total life and personality depended on what Jesus was—and is—and promised to be, and Jesus was willing to freely offer it to the man lying there near the pool of Bethesda.

The words "get up" in the natural realm did not make any sense to the man or to his situation, yet Jesus spoke them. Even though the man's past and the present would seem to disqualify those words, Jesus was declaring that even this man was worthy of a miracle. The long-held tradition of being in the right place at the right time opposes such a claim or promise, but it was necessary for the sake of the invalid man that those words be uttered with power.

After Jesus told him to get up, perhaps the man was thinking, *Are you sure your words are meant for me? Maybe, sir, you didn't hear what I just said to you a moment ago. Please understand, the water is not yet stirred, I don't see any angels, and I'm not the first to enter in it. So please, do not waste your breath and our time.* But when we see our circumstances through the faithful eyes of God and his power, the words become a welcome command to accept God and his plan for us.

The compromised life will never comprehend God's plan in the natural therefore it is necessary to operate in the supernatural. Jesus spoke boldly, "Get up!" He was clearly stating, "I am in control" and "I know what I am doing and why I am doing it." It was important for Jesus to take that stand on that day of the feast at the outskirts of Jerusalem in Bethesda and speak to a man who was neglected for so long. Ignored and forgotten by society but not hidden from the caring and loving eyes of the Creator. Rather than answering with a resounding, "Yes! I want to be healed," the man came up with a reason of why he hadn't been healed. But even so, Jesus did not rescind his offer. He commanded the man to get up. At that time Jesus was rightfully taking back what belonged to God from the enemy who had hijacked and held him captive. This was a huge step for the man, when everything was against him—his health, his failure, his society, his understanding of God—God still believed in him and offered him a miracle. God sees what we fail to see and God sometimes ignores what we see or want to see for our own good and for our miracle.

It is hard for many people to get up from a place of last resort—to get up from our comfort zone and face the uncertainty once again. The power to hold on to what is left is often too strong, but Jesus walks into such scene—a place of fear, confusion, and weakness—and offers the invalid man the greatest hope and strength ever: The hope of a better future, the hope to believe that things can change, the hope that God is for us even when things are against us, and most importantly the hope of becoming what God wants.

Pick Up. Picking up what had been down for a long time is hard enough, but when others don't want it to be picked up or there is little strength left, it becomes extra heavy. Even the thought of making a change becomes so hard that we do not want to do it nor believe that we can do it. The unspoken protocol at the pool was, "We don't do it that way here." Getting up and picking up was not how things were done in that community. Being there for a long time he knew the policies and the system well, so he didn't want to violate it or even offend those who had received the miracle in the usual way by being fast, first, and favored to enter the pool.

Sometimes we are so caught up by protocol that we forget the purpose. Like the invalid man, we become so occupied with how things are done in "Bethesda," that we forget why we are there in the first place. The process of doing things and the way to do things for healing become more important than the healing itself. The usual practices and methods try to choke the very life of the healing that is available from God. Often we get more caught up in *how* to worship than *why* we worship. It is the *why* that takes us to our healing and to our *how*. For the man at the pool, his miracle was standing right in front of him, yet he was undecided, even after repeatedly failing in his attempt to gain his healing or to get his life back. It wasn't easy for him to seize it—that was not the normal method of healing in Bethesda. To renounce the known for the unknown scared him. So when Jesus told the invalid man, "Get up! Pick up your mat and walk," acceptance didn't come easily for him.

Before that shift could occur, a greater shift needed to happen in his thinking, and it had to come from a shift within him. The mat served as an emotional security blanket of sorts that also physically supported him during his life as an invalid. Now Jesus was commanding him to remove it from underneath him. That terrified him. His mat also identified him as an invalid, as a permanent resident of Bethesda, and it wasn't easy for him to give up on it so fast. It was like pulling the carpet out from right under his feet, and that was not a good feeling. He didn't want his known world of thirty-eight years to cave in like that. It was frightening and not an appropriate request from any angle—except when viewed from heaven's angle. Not only that, but picking up the mat meant he was not required to come back to that place ever again.

When Jesus asked him to pick up his mat, it also meant to give up...everything. It required the man to change his attitude and behavior as well as his outlook. This expectation according to his mindset, was too high for which he had no prior experience or information. Jesus was addressing a very significant part of the human condition that often keeps us from moving forward. How often are we even aware that some of the support or support groups or people or systems that supported us and were needed in the past suddenly become burdens when we follow/obey Jesus and his demands? Often our "mats" become weights keeping us in the present, preventing future progress.

It is interesting to note that Jesus was very intentional in having the man pick up the mat and walk; it was symbolic, a reminder to him that he was moving forward and that he was never going back there again—this was not just a momentary phase but something that was permanent. Emptying the space he occupied for many years or giving up an address of your longtime residence can be depressing and cause grief. Picking up and moving means giving up your neighborhood, your friends with whom you barbequed and had block parties, the community where your kids grew up, and things that are familiar, comfortable and understood. It also means breaking off some of the bad company and influence that have the potential to ruin our God-ordained destiny. The man Jesus desired to heal had to put aside many people and things and familiarize himself with a whole new way of life—the life God intended for him.

Picking up and moving forward also meant picking up a new philosophy of life, much different from how he had lived for so long. Now he had to live with a whole new understanding about what he believed and had heard preached. He could not claim that healing comes only for the first, fast, and favored—but was available even for the late and the last. There would be no more stories of survival of the fittest. Rather, his healing was a testimony to all about how an insignificant and helpless person who stood no chance of healing could receive a miracle from a man who entered Bethesda and looked, learned and asked him to pick himself up. It was a new theology of grace. "The last shall be first" was the new slogan of the time.

The healed man had to pick up the hidden dreams that were tucked away under the mat. He had to rethink his ideas about Bethesda, of how to enter the pool to emerge different. Everything had to be looked at in a whole new way. In the initial days he may have jotted in his journal that this was a "temporary situation and I know I will soon be moving forward with my life. Yes, I have been hit hard, but as soon as the pool gets stirred, everyone will know that I don't belong here and am not here to fool around and be part of this community. I'm here as a transient, waiting for my healing to happen." But slowly those pages that were filled initially with so much hope and faith faded, writing about dreams became less and less important until there were no hopes and dreams to write about. His faith, energy, and hope were slowly and steadily sucked out of him as time went on, as years passed by. Dreams gave way to fear and fear slowly turned into acceptance. He accepted the new life of compromise, shattered dreams, and defeated hope.

Picking up those pieces are painful. The mat exposed the truth of his inner soul. Picking up the mat opened new wounds, but this time the healer was standing beside him to hold him and say, because I live, you will live also (See John 14:19). Picking up what cannot be buried is possible if we only believe the one who is able to stand for us; he will help us see a new day.

Walk. Jesus commanded a man to walk who had not walked for thirty-eight years. What was normal, natural and easy for many was hard, painful and impossible for him. What came freely for many, came at a big price for this invalid man. The best way to hide his weakness was to be among others who were weak and become one of them, become part of the invalid group; after all there was support in that group, and people understood him. Being there he didn't have to hide himself, didn't have to explain his condition, he could be visible and be open about his feelings and still be accepted. Being an invalid had become part of who he was—an invalid living by the pool of Bethesda was acceptable. Being among this support group almost made him seem normal. Asking such a person to walk again was abnormal. Getting up, picking up and walking would upend what he had learned to accept. Similarly, after being in a prison environment which is known for being manipulative and deceitful, it would be very difficult for anyone to break free and live a trustworthy life. It would be a difficult walk in that context. Jesus understands his situation but invites him to move beyond into a very different place.

Walking would disqualify the man from getting sympathy or charity anymore. Being accustomed to being helped, shown sympathy, and being taken care of for many years would naturally make it hard for anyone to get back on the path of independence. A life led from the poolside, although it comes with a price, also has its own benefits. The people who cared for the invalids often brought food and cared for them in certain ways, which could be a reason for not wanting to leave. Being dependent kept him at the place of receiving. If he accepted healing to walk, that meant he would be disqualified and turned away from his known world of free food and help. He would be stepping into a place that would force him to fend for himself. It is a fearful place to be when you do not know how to begin.

Walking takes strength in the physical realm but also in the spiritual realm. And that's where Jesus' question was directed, challenging him to give up what was holding him back from taking that step to walk. The road ahead for him also meant stepping into life in a whole new way, including living a productive life by finding a job; there would be no more disability checks coming in. He may have to worry about how to pay the bills, how to get a new driver's license, and other things. All these "normal" issues can become too much for a person who was taken care of by others and didn't know how to fend for himself. So for this man, walking and accepting the miracle of healing, meant taking a giant step. But when Jesus spoke to him, he also meant that he would walk with him and go ahead of him to prepare his way.

This also was a command to the society that had stopped walking in compassion and in the power of God—Jesus was telling them to walk again too, with him. It seemed Jesus was asking a lot from the man and his community because he was willing to pay a heavy price for all humankind. At the same time he was communicating to the world who he is, where his heart is, and that he will be by the man's side, society's side— and our side, always.

> *For an angel went down at a certain time into the pool and stirred up the water; then whoever stepped in first, after the stirring of the water, was made well of whatever disease he had .*
>
> *Now a certain man was there who had an infirmity thirty-eight years. When Jesus saw him lying there, and knew that he already had been in that condition a long time, He said to him, "Do you want to be made well?" Jesus said to him, "Rise, take up your bed and walk." And immediately the man was made well, took up his bed, and walked* (John 5:4-6,8-9).

The moment the paralyzed man obeyed the words Jesus commanded, immediately the man was healed. That day Bethesda witnessed the kind of stirring that not even an angel could offer.

In the next chapter we will see the second meeting of Jesus with the man at a very different place. Jesus did not just heal the man to take him away from Bethesda but journeys with him to help him take away the negative effects of Bethesda from within.

The following chart shows the difference between angelic healing and the healing by Jesus at Bethesda. Jesus brought an entirely new way of healing and relating to those who are suffering. This angered the religious leaders so much that they sought to kill him.

Angelic Healing	Jesus' Healing
You must come to a certain location and wait for it.	Healing comes to where you are, and waits for you.
You have no choice in regard to your healing.	You decide if you want your healing. "Do you want to get well?"
It is a public healing/non-relational.	Very private and highly relational
You must get there by your strength. Healing is for the first, fast and favored ones.	You cannot be healed by your own merit, only by his grace.
You have to keep trying again and again until you get your healing. No guarantees.	You don't have to keep trying. You only have to believe.
Healing is limited to the physical realm.	Healing is holistic; physical as well as spiritual.
You need to know the process, protocol, and place.	Jesus knows the person. He has the plan and a purpose.

Questions to Ponder

Then Jesus said to him, "Get up! Pick up your mat and walk."

1. Get Up

Why was it hard for the man to get up? What are some places we find it difficult to get up from?

2. Pick Up

What was the man's fear of picking up his mat? What are some things that we need to pick up that have been lying down for so long in our life?

3. Walk

Why was it hard for the man to believe that he could walk? What are some things that God is asking us to do that we have never done before?

CHAPTER SEVEN

THE TEMPLE AND SIN

"The peace of God is not the absence of fear. It, in fact, is His presence."
–Tim Keller

And that day was the Sabbath. The Jews therefore said to him who was cured, "It is the Sabbath; it is not lawful for you to carry your bed." He answered them, "He who made me well said to me, 'Take up your bed and walk.'"

Then they asked him, "Who is the Man who said to you, 'Take up your bed and walk'?" But the one who was healed did not know who it was, for Jesus had withdrawn, a multitude being in that place.

Afterward Jesus found him in the temple, and
said to him, "*See, you have been made well. Sin no*
more, lest a worse thing come upon you." *The man*
departed and told the Jews that it was Jesus who had
made him well (John 5:9-15).

The story ends with a strange appearance by Jesus at the temple in Jerusalem. The now-healed man from Bethesda also comes to the temple, perhaps fulfilling a long-awaited dream to be part of the feast in Jerusalem. Has the temple changed since he left, or is it the same as when he was cast out? He waited for thirty-eight years to be free to move around and make his own destiny. Interestingly, he chooses the temple as one of the first places to visit. He is aware of his healing and that he is no longer confined to the suffering crowd of Bethesda, but he is completely ignorant of how he got healed and why.

Jesus finds the healed man and makes a second attempt to connect with him and with his inner self, also to have a conversation about the deeper issue that people at Bethesda deal with on daily basis yet do not want to talk about—sin. The people of Jerusalem do not want to highlight sin either, but from what Jesus told the man, we know sin was one of the reasons that forced people to leave Jerusalem and seek out refuge in Bethesda.

The Temple and the Sin

The temple is where Jesus implored the healed man to seek a deeper understanding of sin and the effects of sin. This place, the temple, where its leaders were slowly, steadily and deliberately avoiding the topic of sin, is where Jesus chose to tell the man about sin. Jesus does not ignore the obvious—he brings the seriousness of sin to the man in a very relational environment. If the temple teachers had been careful to discuss the effects of sin, the man could have learned it from them perhaps years ago. But because the man didn't realize the connection, Jesus had to find him and make him understand.

Sin was one of the primary causes pushing people to Bethesda by making them disabled, paralyzed, and lame. One of the ways Jerusalem was dealing with people's sin was hiding those with visible symptoms at Bethesda. The effect of sin was separating people from their own and keeping them isolated, but there was a more serious consequence that sin could bring into one's life. Jesus highlights it as "a worse thing" that can happen. One of the "worse" things visible in Jerusalem was those who were sick and paralyzed in *spirit* and were not even aware of it or did not feel the spiritual separation, and yet they were active within the temple as if everything was going well. The other "worse" thing was that the people with power controlled the temple and tried to kill Jesus—the one who was able to bring deliverance and healing to the physically sick in

Bethesda and those who were spiritually diseased in Jerusalem. Their religion preached that the sinner has to find dwelling at Bethesda and the only way he can find salvation is through angelic or supernatural stirring—but that came through the man's effort, hard work and resources. Hope for the hopeless was unwelcome and even challenged with death threats.

> *For this reason the Jews persecuted Jesus, and sought to kill Him, because He had done these things on the Sabbath. But Jesus answered them, "My Father has been working until now, and I have been working." Therefore the Jews sought all the more to kill Him, because He not only broke the Sabbath, but also said that God was His Father, making Himself equal with God* (John 5:16-18).

Jewish leaders tried to kill Jesus because he was healing people on the Sabbath. Healing for the Jewish leaders was conditional, and suffering was ignored. Sin finds its roots deep in the religious system, yet people act as if everything is spiritually fine. Sin kills—which is exactly what they tried to do to Jesus.

Physical and Spiritual Healing

The healing of this man was different from the traditional way because for the first time the healing went beyond the physical. His healing started a dialogue among the people about the origin of sin and its effects. It opened a conversation for people to really understand and discuss. It created a chance to talk about sin, the sickness of the soul; and thus, the healing was different for three reasons: 1) Sin is deeper than sickness; 2) Sin affects more than just the person; and 3) No one can forgive sin except Jesus Christ.

The people who were healed at Bethesda often returned to the community and described their experience to others. They might tell the stories of what the diseased and disabled community commonly shared. They also might raise some issues seldom addressed among the people who are forgotten by the majority. But one thing all of them would tell is the story of their healing. Healed people talked about their healing experience because healing did not come easily or to everyone at Bethesda. They might have a detailed report of how they were the fastest or the first to enter the pool on the day the angel came and stirred the water. They would tell others how much preparation or effort was required to receive the healing. The audiences might ponder the work that goes into healing, which few had ever bothered to think about. They might think how privileged they are not to be among those at the poolside.

But then there came a stranger, a healed man among the temple-goers who had a very strange story. Those who had been in Bethesda knew this man, so he was afraid to tell his story of healing because there was no resemblance to others' comeback tales. But what he didn't understand was that one's story with Jesus doesn't have to fit a certain paradigm or be understood by others, because after all Jesus shattered conventional paradigms and was misunderstood. It is said that "he came to his own but his own rejected him" (John 1:11). Jesus left Jerusalem on the day of the feast and walked to a forgotten place and remembered him. As he thought about his experience, he felt that he should speak out. As his testimony was shared, he shocked his audience with a very different theme of healing. It troubled the traditional waters of the religious people of Jerusalem.

The healed man's story didn't include the appearance of an angel, nor was he the first or fastest or favored one; rather, he was so slow that he was unsuccessful for almost four decades. He also didn't describe a time when he saw the water moving. Rather, his story, his healing, was different from any previous healing. This story was not about someone who was just going to heal his physical condition, but someone who was interested in him personally—someone who saw him, learned about him, conversed with him, and genuinely wanted to know him. Moreover, his healing moved beyond the exterior and moved inside him. His healing was personal, relational, and unique—different from all the healing stories ever told about Bethesda. And this story has led people to Jesus and to healing for more than two thousand years, challenging people to leave the traditional experience of life and religion and see and accept the relational nature of God. Many more stories are still being written as people connect with this healer who is compassionately seeking out those who are lost.

1. Sin is deeper than sickness. After the man walked out of Bethesda, his home for thirty-eight years, he is found in the temple, among the religious feast-goers. He is healed, and with healing comes the privilege of being part of the religious community. Although healing opens many new doors for this man, unfortunately along with freedom comes the danger of being trapped in the evil that often preys on a free society—evil that makes people commit sins that disable or paralyze the spirit and the soul, thus enslaving and imprisoning them, even when they think they are free. There are many who when they are inside this prison make a strong commitment to follow and serve the Lord but as they go out into the free world they face the hard reality of life and are often met with rejections due to their past. This often causes them to feel that it is better to go back to their old lifestyle and their old friends who will accept them as they are. Thus, they succumb to the old habits that imprisoned them in the first place.

Although the physical healing was a public event, another healing transpires at the temple. This healing is sacred and concealed. Jesus meets the man at the temple as he is now accepted into society as one among them. He is free to participate and do what he could not do for many years. Unfortunately the man harbored sin within, yet acted as if everything was fine. He knew the effects of physical disability, but he wasn't aware of the disability that sin caused in his spirit.

Jesus makes the effort to meet this man who was now living a new life, his dream life, and warns him of the trap he could fall into if he allows sin to reign in his life. Jesus says to him, *"Sin no more,"* implying that he had committed sin, thus connecting his action and its effects. Jesus helped him account for his every deed and be aware of its impact. Jesus gives this man a different option—a life free from sin. This also means that he had to continue in the habit of getting up, picking up and walking away from sin. He couldn't just move away from it as a one-time event like his physical healing. He needed Jesus' words to support him continually for his spiritual healing.

Perhaps the man wasn't aware that there was a better way to live. But Jesus tells him, "Yes, there is a better way of living—a life free of sin and shame." This was a new concept for this man—and for the community and Jewish society at large. The culture had removed the concept of sin and devalued the theory of sacrifice and sold cheap grace. Now this man had to evaluate whether his actions had violated God's commandment or principle. Now he was given a choice—to live a life pleasing to God or himself and the world.

The free society into which he was reintroduced wasn't prepared to help him see that choice. This is why Jesus met him at the temple during the feast. This man was now trying to live a new life in a new way, but among people who were doing things that were contrary to the commandments of God.

When Jesus meets him, he invites him to see a way of living where he could live without sin and had a choice to *"Sin no more."* He needed to live and lead his life from the inside out. His inner life, hidden from others but open to God, was to be lived in a way that would bring honor and glory to the one who came to him when no one else cared for him. Jesus empowered the man to do things differently—and to make a difference—and thus fulfill his God-given purpose.

2. Sin affects more than just the person. When Jesus visited the temple during the feast and mingled among the faithful Jews and those celebrating the occasion, he told them that part of their family was missing, unaccounted for, hidden and forgotten. He opened their eyes to the lives of those who were marginalized and ignored. He told the stories of those who never had a voice or whose voices were silenced because they were deemed unworthy. He shone his light on this dark corner of the community, not by making loud proclamations or judgmental statements, but by meeting the man who had suffered for so long. Now Jesus wanted to heal those in the community who were more concerned with their celebration than for the poor souls at Bethesda.

The healed man was among the minority in Jerusalem, and his voice would not be heard again. Perhaps he was tempted to be silent, become like the others, forget where he came from and what brought him here, and ignore all those he left behind at the pool. That would be a sin for him, and he would participate in the sin of those in the community who were more concerned about themselves than with those who were hurting. The feast had become all about them, and Jesus saw that the best way to heal the community was to send a man as a witness who knew what suffering can cause, who knew what it means to be forgotten during the feast.

The healed man knew what it meant to miss the joyful celebration and be at a place filled with pain, stink, and anger. He had to speak up. His story gave voice to many who were in Bethesda and were never heard. Our story of brokenness, redemption and relationship with the creator God has to be shared with the world that is lost.

3. No one can forgive sin—except Jesus. This story holds a larger truth. Jesus is visiting the pool of Bethesda when people are more concerned about the feast. They had lost the real meaning of what it means to celebrate life and free all those who are under bondage and imprisonment. He came to preach the good news that there is a hope for all who are blind, disabled, and forgotten. Only Jesus could do that. No angelic stirring ever caused healing that went beyond the physical and touched the heart and spirit of the person and the community. The healing that Jesus brought was not just for the man, but for all. Only he could do it because he came from heaven to earth and entered in the human world which, like Bethesda, is full of suffering, pain, and evil.

Jesus came to set people free of their selfish agendas and teach them about the new way of life and new way of celebrating and fulfilling their purpose To bring a dead soul to life required more than the power of God, it demanded the death of his son on the cross. It meant there needed to be a perfect man willing to hang on the rugged cross with rusted nails holding his hands and feet until he gave up his ghost in exchange for our life.

The healing of the soul demanded God the Father to turn away his compassionate eyes from his only begotten son and allow him to be killed by the Roman soldiers on the hill of Golgotha. The rescue of humanity came at the high price of burying the Son of God in a rented sepulture for three days. Only a sinless man with his precious blood could redeem humanity and show the heart of God to the people who wanted to truly understand what it meant to participate in the feast of God. A sinless God walked into a sinful world to restore it to its rightful place.

Going to Bethesda on the day of the Jewish feast inaugurated God's personal feast and was a celebration of mercy. When we participate in the feast of Jesus as God showed through his son on that day, a new generation of people are influenced and inspired into the ministry and work of God to build his kingdom and restore his mission for his glory.

Estelle Chapel: My mind was still engrossed in everything that Tim shared, about his Bethesda and his new journey of hope and peace. I could barely hold back my tears thinking of the merciful God who walked into the darkness of pain, loneliness and human suffering to see, learn, ask, heal and journey with a man who was broken and lost. I shut my eyes as my ears heard singing from the chapel...*My chains are gone, I've been set free...My God, my Savior has ransomed me...And like a flood his mercy regains, unending love, amazing grace!*

Questions to Ponder

Afterward Jesus found him in the temple, and said to him, "See, you have been made well. Sin no more, lest a worse thing come upon you." The man departed and told the Jews that it was Jesus who had made him well (John 5:9-15).

1. Do you think sin is deeper than any disease? Why?

2. How does sin affect more than just the person?

3. Why do you believe only Jesus can forgive sin?

CHAPTER EIGHT

THE LAST COVERED PORCH

"Teach me to treat all that comes to me with peace of soul and with firm conviction that You will govern all. –Elisabeth Elliot

I was enjoying my ministry as one of the pastors of a beautiful church in the heart of Salt Lake City, Utah. It was not just the exterior that attracted me to this church, but also the interior, the people. Unlike the general demographic of the city, this church had a mix of people from various ethnic backgrounds and nationalities. I was very excited about the opportunity to be part of a dedicated team serving the community. It was very meaningful work, and I relished the compliments I received from the parishioners.

One of my typical days began with visiting three church members living in three different retirement homes. Each visit was extraordinary. Two of them were elderly ladies in their nineties and the third was a man who was approaching his mid-eighties. Not having families nearby to visit made my appointments very special to them. By the time I completed my third visit of the day, I was not only energized but also feeling grateful for the wonderful time I had with these three beautiful people. Listening to their stories and seeing the world from their vantage point, I was gaining a very different perspective on life, faith, family, and future. Their joy was unspeakable in spite of their situation, their faith in God was unshakable beyond any doubt, their spirits were undefeated despite the fatigue that came with age, and their passion and love for community was unfaltering. One had lost her husband when she was still young, yet she remained single for the rest of her life raising kids alone. The other often dealt with difficult health situations, while the man was missing his wife of over sixty years. However, in the midst of their situations, they still found joy in small things such as playing cards with their housemates, enjoying a dish of ice cream, and offering prayer with their spiritual community. Their smiles and stories encouraged me to look forward to our next visit.

The same evening also allowed me to be part of a young adults group from the church which met at a posh restaurant. Most of them were working their dream jobs: a pilot, a nurse, a psychologist, an investment banker, a research scientist, to name a few professions. We talked about dreams, faith, struggles, life, and a bit about family. I listened to their stories, periodically interjecting with some of my experiences on my own journey. I thoroughly enjoyed being part of this group that was trying to live out its faith in an unfavorable culture, and at the same time desperately searching for help to stand up against various inner struggles.

By the time we ended our day, the street lights had illuminated the silent city outside and a few temple-goers were now finding their way back home. I walked to the parking lot, got into my car and on the empty freeway—thinking how blessed I was that I had been entrusted with a ministry with such awesome folks in a beautiful city that was a religious center. It felt like I was at the right place at the right time, and looking down the road things were looking pretty good. It was almost like being among the feast-goers.

I pulled into our driveway; humming to myself. I entered the house and soon my two beautiful daughters were hugging me tightly with pure excitement and holding me firmly with their small hands. They led me to the dinner table where my wife had prepared a delicious meal for all of us. I sat down and closed my eyes to thank the good Lord for my family, faith, and the feast I was going to enjoy. My youngest one finished praying for the meal and the rest of them waited for me to open my eyes. I opened them as my wife gently placed her hand on my back and my two girls were giggling. Then my wife said to me, "There is a surprise…I received an offer from a university in Texas."

As her words fell on my ears, I saw them waiting for my reaction with their eyes like wide circles. Without thinking about it I said, "Wow, that's great news. I think you should take it." I knew the girls weren't going to be happy to make a move, but I also knew it was an opportunity for my wife to advance her clinical psychological practice. At the same time, I wasn't prepared to give up my ministry and walk away from it. What we also didn't know was that the town we were moving to was not considered family-friendly. It was unlike any other place we'd lived; it was a city surrounded by prisons. A place where the social invalids lived within walls. We were moving from a religious center to a prison center. To say the least, the move was hard and it was exhausting for all of us to get settled. It took a long time for us to adjust and the girls found it difficult to fit in.

Fitting In

While my wife was slowly settling into her new job, I was visiting local churches, looking for any ministry opportunity. During the process, I was surprised that the make-up of many churches did not represent the mix of people who made up the town. Another surprise was when God led me to minister in the prisons. This opened my mind and my heart to a whole new level of understanding people, their stories, and pain. It was a ministry in which I had no real experience, but I was prepared to follow God's lead.

The first time I walked into a penitentiary, I noticed that the offenders were of different shapes, sizes, colors, and backgrounds—but with common crime stories, along with pain and fear, far removed from the normal pace and lifestyles of free society. The barbed wire fence surrounding the prison made it very clear that no one could enter or depart without authorization. The divide between the two worlds was huge. No one would enter voluntarily.

Most prisons are located away from the "nice neighborhoods," hidden from the community, as if by ignoring them they could forget them. It may not be intentional, but it was comfortable. Though the people I met in the neighboring community didn't want to talk about the prison, I found that in their midst there were those living with shame, pain, and loneliness, the consequences of their own crimes or the crimes of loved ones who were locked up. Many crimes leave behind painful wounds on the victims and change their lives forever.

The families of criminals live with unspeakable misery and pain. There are elderly parents with sad memories of the son they disowned because of crime; his empty chair at the table is a constant reminder that his story was cut short and there will be no happy ending. Likewise, empty chairs belonging to fathers, mothers, sisters, and brothers silently scream at every Thanksgiving dinner and every family gathering. At the same time, inside the prison walls, those incarcerated know the wrong choices they made and that they didn't fit well within the demands of the community. They know that they are despised and discarded—but some are trying to make the best of their lives and times. There are also a few who know that their prison sentence has given them an opportunity to change their ways and return to those empty chairs they left behind.

Now and then someone leaves the prison, goes back into the community, and tries to live his dream—just like those leaving Bethesda. This gives those left behind hope, hope enough to wait for their time to get out and get back to normal life in the free world. But, like the man beside the pool for thirty-eight years, there are a few who are left behind in prison who have tried and tried, yet fail repeatedly to receive help at the right time. Perhaps they were not granted parole numerous times and had to accept the hard fact that they are never going to get out of prison. And there are those who know that they don't want to repeat what they have done in the past and want to desperately change their life but have repeatedly failed to do so. Consequently, they make their own meaning of prison life and their community, and accept who and where they are.

I came here not knowing what lay ahead for me. But one thing was clear, this place was very different from the place I left some months ago. It was nothing like the beautiful, shining city I had left behind, where people spent time celebrating family, faith, and feasts together. Here the brokenness was visible, the loneliness obvious, the hurting evident, and the pain widespread. For the offender, the victim, the children, the church, and the community at large it is a heavy burden emotionally and physically, as well as financially. The aching questions are: Is there a way out? Will they stay by the poolside wishing and hoping for an angel to stir the water? Or will they seek the one who is ready, willing, and able to heal them emotionally, relationally, mentally, physically, and spiritually? The question for the community is will we wait for an angelic appearance or settle only for a supernatural manifestation? Will we respond with "yes" when he asks us, "Do you want to be healed?" or do we give excuses and stay in our own Bethesda?

Being a pastor to prisoners made me ask a few questions: How do most people deal with hurt, pain, and suffering? Is it possible to ignore or hide the pain, removing it far from us? Is healing only for the outcast, or do our communities need healing too? When we send those disabled by their crime to live among themselves as in Bethesda, are we removing ourselves far from them? Many of these questions will never be answered or will ever make any sense at all on this side of eternity.

More about Tim

Tim was sitting in my office sharing the rest of his life story and carefully backtracking to every event that brought him to his current situation. He was cautious in making sense of some of the life choices he had made that led him to places where he never wanted to be and ultimately prison. He had tried his best to fit in. "My religion failed me and my own didn't help me. I didn't know what to do." According to him, he didn't have it in himself to be able to make it there, and that's when he tried to find those who would accept him just as he was, his group, his people. But that was not the answer. People who accepted him and invited him in were the same broken people living the same broken lives.

After a while he gave up trying to be normal and just accepted who he was and gave up everything just to be part of that group. The force to belong is compelling enough for people to abandon relationships; and the fear of being left out is strong enough to cause people to reject what is right or good. During this process, Tim told me that life was hard, painful, and more confusing. Finding himself in a prison environment gave him an opportunity to rediscover himself. Although it was a place that was creating a new—hopefully better—identity, it was also adding frustration and pain that he was suppressing inside.

Tim hoped one day to be restored to normal life with a normal family in a normal community. It was a struggle for Tim to be in a violent environment and be lonely and abandoned by his own people. Even the friendships that he forged inside the prison walls weren't giving him the peace or meaning he was searching for. It took years for him to understand why people like him were shunned or removed from society. He didn't function as they wanted him to, which made him think that he wasn't good enough for them. So the best way to deal with that mindset was to hate all who were on the other side of the barbed wire, and embrace all the people who were inside. But that wasn't helping him.

According to Tim, he had almost given up on life. He felt enveloped in total darkness with no way of getting out. That's when something strange happened. One of his cellmates talked about God one day, which made him very upset because he thought religion and faith belonged to those in the outside world, and anything coming from there was no good. Nevertheless, Tim didn't say a word and didn't instigate a fight like he had in the past.

Tim was so totally against God and the people who believed in him that he didn't even think it was worth fighting over. But somehow what his cellmate said lingered in his mind.

A couple of weeks later most of the religious inmates were gone for some Saturday services and he was alone in his cell late, thinking about God. He asked a question, "God, I don't believe in you and I don't think you are real…but if what the other dude was saying is true, please show yourself to me." He didn't even know if his words made any sense at all.

Light in the Darkness

According to Tim, in the early hours of the morning when everything around him was dark, there shone a bright light with an appearance of a figure, who can only be compared to an angel. Then he heard a voice that sounded like thunder yet was as soothing as a calm sea. He saw the compassionate eyes of one who had left his throne to be with him, searched deep inside his soul and asked a question, "Do you want to get well?" Tim could not believe what he was experiencing, he thought he was dreaming. But he was very aware of being awake and knew that what he was seeing and hearing was true. Tears rolled down from his eyes. For the very first time he was feeling something in his heart, which had been hardened and calloused for many long years…almost thirty-eight years. He couldn't go back to sleep. He lay silent but awake…weeping and soaking in the love of the one who came to meet him. As he pulled himself up from the steel bed, the sun was coming up over the prison, the bright rays were breaking forth from the darkness, he felt a new strength within him and peace around him that he had never felt before.

The encounter with God that night caused Tim to see things in a very different light. He had never heard God speak before and had never read scriptures, but he knew his experience of God was real. The next day, he looked for the inmate who had first talked to him about God. He borrowed his Bible, and for the next few days read and absorbed God's word. As he started flipping through the pages of this ancient sacred text, his eyes fell on the Gospel of John, chapter 5 and it began to stir him from the inside out. He couldn't believe that something of that nature could be possible. All his life he had heard, known and believed that God was distant and unapproachable. But he read the story of the man from Bethesda and he gained a whole new understanding of who he is and was and his concern for one man. He couldn't sleep and spent the night ruminating on this experience.

A new spirit was birthed within Tim. He couldn't explain the peace, joy, and life he was experiencing. For the very first time, he was not filled with hate for people, instead there was a deep sense of compassion and peace. He met with the chaplain and started attending church services. He shared his experience and his faith with people around him and enrolled himself in various faith-based classes. Soon he discovered that God was real, and in his words he "found meaning and purpose" for his life. He also started sharing what he was experiencing with his family who had abandoned him long ago. None of his family replied, except his dad who was the only member of his family to keep in touch with Tim.

Tim's dad would visit him once in a while. Now when he came to visit, Tim would share about his new life and the faith he had discovered, telling him how God met him and set him free and gave him a new life. He would tell his dad how God renewed his life and gave him hope. But his testimony didn't seem to affect his dad; he was old and wanted to enjoy the rest of his years without being bothered by his son's God stories. He always told his son, "I would rather enjoy golf on Sunday mornings than anything else." But about a year into their conversations about God, his dad wrote to him and asked him about faith, his fears and his own personal spiritual struggles. Tim was surprised and told him that he would be glad to share what he knew the next time he came to visit.

Tim's dad visited the very next week and asked Tim to tell him more about God. His dad even asked Tim to pray for him to experience the same joy and peace that Tim was experiencing. Tim was a little skeptical, so he kept the conversation about God till the end of the visit, but he could see that his dad was getting uneasy and he kept pressing him to share and pray with him. Finally, Tim told his dad about God's love and his forgiveness and his promise to give all those who believe in him a new life. Before his dad left, Tim prayed for him and they hugged each other. As his dad departed, Tim could see brightness in his dad's teary eyes.

Tim went back to his cell and went to bed a little early. Very early the next morning he was called by the chaplain to come see him. He didn't know what to expect, and couldn't believe what he heard. The chaplain told Tim that his dad had a major heart attack the previous evening while having dinner at home. Though he was rushed to the hospital by an ambulance, he died on the way. Tim slowly sat down to process carefully what he was hearing from the chaplain.

His heart skipped a beat, but in that moment he also felt the comforting peace of his Savior next to him, telling him that he was with him even when life doesn't make sense.

Tim's eyes filled with tears as he told me this story. He said he felt a strange sense of peace knowing that his dad was in the presence of the Lord. He was surprised that his dad just the day before made that important decision to follow the Lord and trust him with his whole heart—and within a few hours he was gone. He knew that his dad would meet the Savior who once came to visit him in his dark prison cell. He was comforted in knowing that his father was now resting in the arms of his everlasting Father. Though the loss didn't make sense, still the hope of seeing his dad again one day filled his heart with great peace.

Tim told me that when he walked back to his cell he felt like God was holding him in his hands and saying that he was making him a blessing to those who are separated from him and far away. I was listening to this story of an amazing transformation of a man who did not meet the standards of society, but now found a new standard that God set for him and made for him for his own purpose. One who was lost was now found.

Tim left my office, but before he left he shared the following three points with me in closing: crowd, Sabbath and work. I feel it connects well with the Bethesda story.

The Crowd

Jesus didn't stay at Bethesda. Healing for Jesus was more than attention-seeking or self-promotion—it was a compassionate move to show the Jerusalem dwellers the real meaning of the feast. Instead of using the crowd to heighten his visibility, Jesus uses the crowd to hide. Drawing a crowd was not the end goal for the man's healing. But drawing suffering and hurting humanity to God was.

Tim told me that is what Jesus did in his life. In the midst of the crowd, Jesus saw him, learned about him, asked about him, healed him and walked with him. Tim said he has decided to be a person who is not going after fame and a crowd pleasing life anymore, rather he will be a person who will seek

God and do his will among the people. He felt like the man from Bethesda who was healed and now was compelled to go and share the saving grace of the Savior Jesus to those who were lying near the pool—waiting for an angel or religion to save them.

Sabbath

Jesus gave new meaning to the Sabbath by restoring the man to the temple, to his people and to the feast. He made the Sabbath not a hindrance but a deliverance to hurting people. This was powerful because religion had separated people from what was real: people's needs and their suffering. And many where getting frustrated and tired of an uncaring religion. Tim said his life was changed because of the compassionate relationship God established with him so personally. He said the Sabbath now had a new meaning for him because that was when Christ stretched his hands to mend the brokenness. Tim emphasized that it is not religion and tradition that people need but a relationship with the Creator God who is seeking those who are lost. Though he lived within the prison walls, he is now able to touch others like the one who touched him.

Work

Jesus displayed the work ethic of his Father who is always at work, who never stops working, and thus he himself is inspired to work. Jesus gave work a new meaning. Work brings healing, teaches us about sin, and restores people into the community. Work done only to generate profit or build one's own empire by promoting tradition or religion, without understanding human suffering, is not work according to Jesus.

As he departed, Tim said that his life was dedicated to work for his Lord and for the one who did not stop working to change him, save him and the one who met him when the rest of the world had stopped working for him. He said that his life's mission was to work as Christ did and never stop until everyone that God brings in his path has heard about the one who sees, learns, asks, and walks with us to heal us of our brokenness and seat us at the empty chair in his Father's house.

With those words still fresh in my mind, I focused on the road ahead toward my home. The darkness was thick yet the house was brightly lit. I walked in straight to the dinner table where my family was eagerly waiting for me. As I sat on my chair, I took a deep breath and without thinking said, "He surely fills the empty chair." Then we broke bread as a family.

Bibliography

Barton, R. Ruth. *Strengthening the Soul of Your Leadership: Seeking God in the Crucible of Ministry.* Downers Grove, IL: IVP Books, 2008.

Benefiel, Margaret. *The Soul of a Leader: Finding Your Path to Fulfillment and Success.* New York: Crossroad Publishing Co., 2008.

Maxwell, John C. *The 21 Most Powerful Minutes in a Leader's Day: Revitalize Your Spirit and Empower Your Leadership.* Nashville, TN: Thomas Nelson Publishers, 2000.

Nouwen, Henri J. M. *In the Name of Jesus: Reflections on Christian Leadership.* New York: Crossroad, 1989.

ABOUT THE AUTHOR

James Levi is a Christian minister who regularly conducts retreat and workshops. He was born and raised in India. After completing his master's degree in biochemistry, he worked in the healthcare industry. Later, he felt called to pursue his calling. His Ph.D. is in international development with a specialization in leadership.

He is a licensed pilot who loves making coffee for his wife and spending time with his two daughters.

James Levi's other books are available on Amazon and you can also check his blogs and vlogs at www.jameslevi.org

38 at Estelle

www.ingramcontent.com/pod-product-compliance
Lightning Source LLC
Chambersburg PA
CBHW021125020426
42331CB00005B/627